RETHINK EVERYTHING

TOMMY CLIFFORD

Cover & *layout by* Princess Hannah Arsenio

RETHINK
EVERYTHING

TOMMY CLIFFORD

CONTENTS

CONTENTS

Foreword

I was standing on the back porch, frozen in the late November air, tears streaming down my face. I had slipped away quietly, hoping no one would notice—the last thing I wanted was for my family to see me like this. Inside, they huddled together, talking and laughing, their voices bubbling up excitedly. My little ones were sprawled out on the floor, building Lego towers and making up adventures, wholly lost in their world of imagination. They were talking about Christmas—the gifts they were hoping for, the holiday movies they couldn't wait to watch, the cookies we'd bake together. Their laughter was carefree, their spirits light, each word filled with the expectation that everything they dreamed of would come to life.

To them, I was just Dad—the one who could always make things happen. They didn't know that, at that moment, I felt like an imposter in my own life. I wanted so badly to join them, to feel that same warmth and joy. But I couldn't do it. I couldn't pretend that I wasn't terrified. Instead, I stood on the porch, feeling the bite of the Alaskan winter against my skin, hoping the cold would somehow numb the ache in my heart. I felt like I was suffocating, unable to breathe under the crushing weight of the truth I was hiding from them.

The truth was, I had nothing lined up. No deals. No clients. No pipeline. Nothing. Despite all the years I'd spent in business, I'd neglected something critical that left me in the cold, gripped by a deep, gnawing hopelessness. I'd built a career, but I hadn't built a foundation. I had no way to make their Christmas dreams come true or give them the holiday they deserved. I was drowning in regret, cursing myself for every choice I'd made, every moment I'd put off building a solid base for my business, hoping that somehow, things would just work out.

At that moment, I felt like a failure—not just as a business owner but a father. I couldn't shake the fear that I was letting them down in ways they didn't understand. I was supposed to be the provider, the one who made things possible, who built their dreams alongside my own. But I was empty. Hollow. Standing on that porch, I felt like there was nowhere to go, no next step, no hope on the horizon.

Maybe you know that feeling. Perhaps you've had those nights when you lie awake, wondering how you will keep it all together. I wonder if you've missed something crucial or if there's a better way to build this life you've poured everything into. After coaching more than 7,000 business owners, I can tell you this is more common than you'd think. The biggest regret I hear, time and time again, is this:

"I wish I'd built my database sooner. I wish I'd taken care of my CRM. I wish I'd created something stable and could rely on."

If you're holding this book, know this: you don't have to stand alone on that cold porch. You're not on this journey alone. This book is here to guide you and ensure you have the foundation I wished I'd had. It's not just a guide. It's a lifeline. The map can lead you from hopelessness to stability, from scarcity to freedom.

Being able to coach and work alongside Thomas Clifford, Mike Frahm, Bree Caddell, and Larry Hales, I have seen firsthand the results and impact these principles—along with the wisdom of this book's authors—can have on real lives and businesses. I've watched countless individuals transform their businesses, going from anxious and uncertain to confident and empowered. I've seen these systems work in theory, practice, and real people's lives. And now, that transformation is available to you.

Inside these pages, you'll find more than just strategies. You'll find the steps to transform your database and CRM into the heartbeat of your business—a foundation that gives you stability, growth, and peace of mind. You don't have to wonder if your company will survive the following season. You don't have to live with the fear of an empty pipeline, the dread of an uncertain future. This book is here to help you create a business that isn't just profitable but predictable—a business that serves you, supports you, and gives back to you.

Imagine stepping into each new season knowing you have a business that sustains you, that you're building a legacy for your family, and that you're free to spend time with them without worry or fear. This is the life you can create—one that fills your heart instead of weighing it down.

So, who is this book for? It's for anyone tired of the chase and ready to build something that endures. It's for every entrepreneur wanting to step away from the grind and create a legacy. If you've ever felt the weight of uncertainty or wished for something solid to stand on, this book is your answer.

Dive in. This book is your gift to yourself. It answers the question, "How can I make this last?" Let it guide you, empower you, and remind you that you have the power to create a future filled not with fear or scarcity but with stability, growth, and unshakeable confidence.

The best way to predict the future is to create it. This is your moment to escape the cold and build the life and business you've always wanted.

It's time to Be Your Hero.

WAYNE SALMANS
Business Coach
Hero Nation Coaching

INTRODUCTION

 Throughout my life, I've always been curious about how things work. Whether it's a new piece of software or an entire system, I've had an unquenchable thirst for learning and understanding. That curiosity has driven me from early college to where I am today, inspiring me to write this book.

I vividly remember walking into a local bookstore back in college, picking up two books on desktop publishing—one for Adobe Illustrator 1.1 and another for QuarkXPress 3.2. I had no formal training or prior experience, but that didn't stop me. I dove in headfirst, teaching myself how to use these tools, mastering them one page at a time. Soon, I added Adobe Photoshop and PageMaker to my skillset. I wasn't just learning software—I was learning systems, breaking down processes, and putting them back together. I was becoming, in a sense, a digital tinkerer.

One of my earliest digital adventures came with my first Macintosh IIsi, which I purchased with a Pell Grant. That computer had something on it called HyperCard—a piece of software that, in retrospect, was my first real CRM. It was more than just an address book. I used it to keep track of everything from contacts to recipes. It fascinated me how I could organize and access information in one place whenever needed. It was a small but significant taste of what would become a lifelong passion for digital

Rethink Everything

organization.

Fast-forward to my career in the printing and prepress industry, where I continued to dig deeper into systems and processes. I became the go-to person for figuring out workflows and creating standard operating procedures so clients could send us files consistently and repeatedly. It wasn't just about solving problems but about making complex systems simple and easy to use.

This passion for simplifying the complex ultimately led to my fascination with CRM systems. Until a few years ago, businesses were using a mishmash of tools: Excel spreadsheets for customer databases, separate email marketing software, and different surveys and forms platforms. Managing customer relationships across these fragmented systems was a nightmare. If a customer opted out of one communication tool, their information wouldn't sync across the others, leading to chaos and confusion.

Enter CRM—specifically, all-encompassing CRM platforms that bring everything together in one place. The ability to manage customer data, automate processes, and integrate various tools into one central hub was a game-changer. The more I dug into CRMs, the more I realized their potential to transform businesses, and that's what captivated me.

It wasn't long before my business partner, Mike, and I recognized the same digital sprawl in many of the

businesses we worked with. We saw people bumping into walls, using half a dozen different tools to manage customer relationships without any real strategy. That's when we decided to create So Easy Solutions, a platform designed to simplify the chaos and help businesses harness the power of a well-organized CRM. I proudly wear the title of Chief Problem Solver, and that's what this book is all about—helping you solve the problems that come with managing customer relationships in today's digital world.

I've always believed that if I'm the smartest person in the room, I'm hanging out in the wrong room. That's why I've surrounded myself with brilliant collaborators— people with unique perspectives on CRM, digital tools, and business strategy. This book isn't just my story. It's a collection of insights from other experts, each bringing their take on how CRMs can revolutionize how we interact with customers.

CRMs mean different things to different people. For some, it's a tool for managing sales leads. For others, it's about nurturing long-term customer relationships. This book showcases the diverse capabilities of modern CRMs, from automation to analytics, and I hope you find a chapter that speaks directly to your business needs. Whether you're just starting out with CRM or looking to refine your existing system, this book will guide you to executing at an elite level.

I am deeply thankful to the collaborators who contributed their knowledge and expertise to this project, especially Kyle Draper, whose guidance was instrumental in bringing this book to life. I'm also grateful to my family, business partners, and the incredible team at So Easy Solutions for their unwavering support.

CRMs are more than just software—they're the key to building more robust, more meaningful relationships with your customers. And that's why I wrote this book. I hope that by the time you finish reading, you'll have the tools and insights you need to harness the full potential of your CRM and take your business to the next level.

TOMMY CLIFFORD

Join the
*Rethink Everything You Need
to Know About A CRM* HERE

Rethink Everything

CHAPTER 1:

The Roots of CRM:
From Rolodex to Digital Dynamo

Customer Relationship Management (CRM) might sound like a recent buzzword in business tech, but managing customer relationships is far from new. The CRM journey started long before software companies turned it into a multi-billion-dollar industry. Today, CRMs are sophisticated platforms that manage everything from sales pipelines to customer service, but it wasn't always this way.

To understand how we got here, we need to travel back to the days when customer relationships were managed with Rolodexes, not digital dashboards. This chapter explores the fascinating evolution of

CRM, from its humble beginnings as a simple way to manage contacts to the powerful, AI-powered platforms we rely on today.

THE EARLY DAYS—ROLODEX, NOTEPADS, AND GUT INSTINCT

Before we had sleek, cloud-based CRMs capable of automating tasks and generating predictive analytics, customer relationship management looked much more…manual. Picture this: a cluttered desk covered in sticky notes, a physical Rolodex packed with business cards, and a frazzled salesperson trying to remember which client needed a follow-up call.

Back in the day, this was CRM.

Salespeople and business owners kept track of their customers by sheer force of will (and a lot of paper). Relationships were managed by memory, personal notebooks, and sometimes even a trusty assistant. Every customer interaction was stored in someone's brain or scribbled down on a notepad. The process was informal, messy, and prone to human error.

But despite its flaws, this old-school approach laid the groundwork for what was to come. The goal was the same: to maintain and grow relationships with customers. However, as businesses grew and customer bases expanded, it became clear that gut instinct and paper records wouldn't cut it.

THE FIRST CRM SYSTEMS— ENTER THE DIGITAL ERA

By the late 1980s and early 1990s, the digital revolution was starting to reshape the business world. As companies grew more prominent and customer interactions became more complex, businesses began to see the need for a more structured way to manage customer information. Enter the first CRM systems.

ACT! and GoldMine: The Pioneers

Two early contenders in the CRM space were ACT! and GoldMine. These programs were digital versions of the Rolodex, offering a way to store contact information and notes about customer interactions. While rudimentary by today's standards, these systems were revolutionary at the time.

ACT!, for instance, was one of the first software solutions that allowed businesses to store and retrieve customer contact details, track communication history, and manage sales opportunities—all in one place. GoldMine took it a step further by offering additional features like email integration and tracking sales leads.

These early systems were designed for individual users or small sales teams, and they gave businesses a glimpse of what was possible when customer data was organized and centralized. But they were still limited. At the end of the day, they were more like glorified address books than the comprehensive CRMs we know today.

THE RISE OF CLOUD-BASED CRMS— SALESFORCE CHANGES THE GAME

In the late 1990s, something big happened— something that would change CRM forever. Salesforce entered the scene, and with it came the birth of the cloud-based CRM. For the first time, businesses could manage customer relationships without having to install expensive software on their local machines.

Why the cloud was a Game-changer

Before cloud-based CRMs, businesses had to rely on on-premise software, which meant high upfront costs, complicated installations, and the constant headache of maintaining the system. But Salesforce changed all that by offering CRM as a service, accessible from any internet-connected device.

With Salesforce, businesses could store all of their customer data in the cloud, making it accessible to sales teams, customer service reps, and marketing departments—anywhere, anytime. No more spreadsheets, no more fragmented data, no more relying on a single office computer to manage customer relationships. The cloud made CRM collaborative, scalable, and infinitely more efficient.

But it wasn't just the technology that made Salesforce stand out—it was the mindset shift. Salesforce was one of the first companies to position CRM as a strategic asset, not just a sales tool. It was about building deeper relationships with customers, predicting their needs, and using data to drive business growth.

MODERN CRM SYSTEMS—INTEGRATION, AUTOMATION, AND PERSONALIZATION

Fast forward to today, and CRM systems have evolved far beyond their contact management roots. Modern CRMs like HubSpot, Zoho, and Microsoft Dynamics are powerful platforms that integrate with virtually every aspect of a business—from sales and marketing to customer service and operations.

Integration

Today's CRMs don't just manage customer contact information—they integrate with email marketing tools, social media platforms, e-commerce systems, and even accounting software. This integration allows businesses to track every touchpoint with a customer, from the moment they first visit your website to the time they make a purchase (and beyond).

Automation

Automation has also become a cornerstone of modern CRM systems. CRMs can now handle tasks like sending follow-up emails, assigning leads to salespeople, and even setting reminders for customer service reps to check in with clients. These automated workflows save time, reduce errors, and ensure that no customer interaction slips through the cracks.

Personalization

Perhaps the most exciting development in modern CRMs is the ability to deliver personalized experiences at scale. Thanks to the massive amounts of customer data stored in CRM systems, businesses can now tailor their marketing messages, sales pitches, and customer service interactions to individual preferences and behaviors. From personalized email campaigns to customized product recommendations, CRMs are helping businesses create meaningful, one-to-one relationships with their customers—on a massive scale.

THE FUTURE OF CRM— AI AND PREDICTIVE ANALYTICS

As we look to the future, the next big frontier in CRM is artificial intelligence (AI). While AI is already being used in some CRM platforms, the potential for growth is enormous.

AI-Powered CRMs

Imagine a CRM that doesn't just track customer data but actually analyzes it to predict future behavior. AI-powered CRMs can help businesses anticipate customer needs, recommend the best times to reach out, and even automate personalized communications based on past interactions.

Predictive analytics is another area where CRMs are poised to revolutionize customer relationships. By analyzing historical data, CRMs will soon be able to predict which leads are most likely to convert, which customers are at risk of churning, and which products or services will appeal to different customer segments.

CONCLUSION:
FROM ROLODEX TO DIGITAL DYNAMO

The evolution of CRM from a simple Rolodex to a sophisticated digital platform is a testament to how far businesses have come in managing customer relationships. What started as a way to keep track of contact information has evolved into a critical business strategy, helping companies build deeper, more meaningful relationships with their customers. As we move into the future, CRMs will continue to evolve, driven by advancements in AI, automation, and data integration. But no matter how advanced these systems become, one thing will remain the same: at the heart of CRM is the goal of understanding and serving the customer better. And as long as businesses stay true to that mission, CRMs will remain one of the most powerful tools for growth and success.

CHAPTER 2:

Building Blocks: The Essential CRM Blueprint

Imagine a business built on strong customer relationships—an organization not just driven by transactions but by trust, loyalty, and shared values. The key to achieving this is understanding the journey every customer takes and optimizing every interaction along the way. The engine that drives this forward? A Customer Relationship Management (CRM) system, the cornerstone of sustainable business growth.

At the core of every successful business is the ability to build lasting relationships. Relationships are built on trust, and trust is earned over time, through consistency, understanding, and personalized experiences. A CRM is not just a tool but a philosophy that allows businesses to nurture these relationships at scale. It's the foundation that transforms one-time customers into lifelong advocates.

My first entrepreneurial endeavor was selling dirt as a four-year-old. I dug up dirt from my backyard, packaged it into plastic grocery bags, and set up a stand to sell to neighbors. Like many small businesses, I focused solely on acquiring new customers. After convincing a few of my neighbors to purchase (what was readily available in their backyards), I was focused on getting people to walk up the driveway to my stand, not realizing I could have nurtured the few customers I had—including my grandparents—into becoming repeat buyers.

The lesson here? Backyard topsoil is not a great product. But more importantly, businesses often overlook the power of nurturing existing customers in favor of the pursuit of new ones. A CRM is the solution to this. It helps you track who has already trusted you, ensuring you're not missing opportunities to deepen that trust.

For the last 5 years, I've had the privilege of helping over 6000 businesses adopt and implement a new CRM into their business. From businesses making their first thousand dollars to businesses doing over $50M annually, I've seen firsthand that a CRM is the backbone of predictable success. What I'm sharing with you is the result of thousands of conversations and implementations. I've also been fortunate to conduct the largest comprehensive survey of these business owners to identify the key growth drivers that a CRM provides. Find me on Instagram @ mattdeseno and DM me the word "CRM" if you'd like to get that PDF report for free.

Ultimately, a CRM is a tool to facilitate growth. To determine what an effective and impactful CRM will look like for your business, you must understand three principles: how your business grows, how your customers grow, and how CRMs work.

PRINCIPLE I

The Two Paths to Growth: More Customers or Higher Value Customers

There are two primary ways to grow a business: acquire new customers or increase the value of existing ones. While both are important, the latter is often more straightforward. Yet, many businesses focus almost exclusively on the former.

The real question we need to ask is not, "How do we get more customers?" but, "How do we provide more value to the customers we already have?"

A well-implemented CRM allows you to map out and enhance the customer journey—building trust at every touchpoint and ensuring each interaction adds value. It transforms a basic transaction into a meaningful connection.

PRINCIPLE 2

The Two Paths to Growth: More Customers or Higher Value Customers

The CRM is the engine behind what's known as the "customer flywheel." This model moves customers through four distinct stages: from strangers to prospects, from prospects to customers, and from customers to promoters. Each stage feeds the next, creating a self-sustaining cycle of growth.

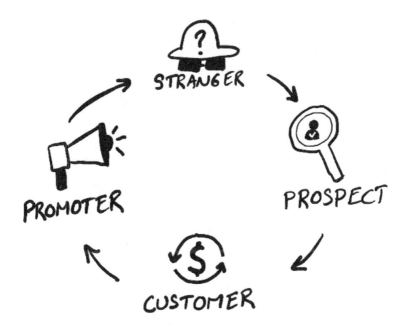

Think of a stranger who visits your website—they're intrigued, but not yet committed. The CRM tracks their behavior, allowing you to understand their needs and offer personalized follow-ups. If done well, they become a prospect, and eventually a customer. Once you've earned their trust and delivered exceptional value, they become promoters of your brand, bringing new strangers into your orbit. The CRM keeps this flywheel spinning smoothly, without extra effort.

PRINCIPLE 3
*Visibility, Accountability, and Automation: The
Three Pillars of CRM Success*

To break down how a CRM works, let's focus on three key components that a CRM amplifies: visibility, accountability, and automation.

Visibility: Knowing Your Customer
A CRM gives you visibility into your entire customer ecosystem. From strangers who land on your website to long-time customers, it provides data that's critical for making informed decisions.

You can see where prospects are in the sales pipeline, which campaigns are converting, and even predict which customers are likely to churn. This level of insight turns what used to be guesswork into a science.

Accountability: Ensuring Follow-Through

A CRM system makes your entire team (and you!) accountable. No longer can a lead fall through the cracks, nor can a loyal customer be ignored post-purchase. Every interaction is logged, every promise tracked.

In business, the speed at which you respond to leads can be the difference between success and failure. A well-cited Harvard Business Review study[1] revealed that businesses which respond to leads within the first hour have a 7x greater chance of having a conversation with a decision maker, and businesses that responded in 5 minutes or less had a 400x greater conversion rate than businesses that responded in 10 minutes. A CRM ensures no opportunity is missed, holding your team accountable for timely responses and quality interactions.

Automation: Scaling Personalization

Perhaps the most magical element of a CRM is its ability to automate processes without losing the personal touch. From automated emails that follow up with leads to drip campaigns that educate customers, automation allows you to stay connected and engaged at scale.

For example, after a customer completes a purchase, an automated sequence can send personalized thank-you emails, onboard them with helpful resources, and request feedback—all without requiring manual effort.

[1] Oldroyd, James B., Kristina McElheran, and David Elkington. "The Short Life of Online Sales Leads." Harvard Business Review 89, no. 3 (March 2011).

THE IMPORTANCE OF CUSTOMER EXPERIENCE

A CRM isn't just about managing contacts; it's about managing experiences. Every interaction your customer has with your brand should be intentional and crafted to exceed expectations.

We often put so much energy into acquiring new customers that we forget about the ones we already have. With a CRM, you can orchestrate a seamless post-purchase experience that keeps customers delighted long after they've handed over their payment.

TURNING CUSTOMERS INTO PROMOTERS

The most successful businesses don't just have customers; they have promoters—people who actively champion your brand and bring in new business. But turning customers into promoters doesn't happen by accident. It requires a system that tracks engagement, measures satisfaction, and proactively encourages feedback.

One of the simplest ways to do this is by asking for reviews at the right moment. A CRM can automate this process, sending a request after a customer has had a positive interaction with your business. Positive reviews are the lifeblood of any growing company, and a CRM ensures you capture them at the peak of your customer's satisfaction.

CONCLUSION: BUILDING YOUR BLUEPRINT

The building blocks of a successful CRM strategy are simple but powerful: visibility, accountability, and automation. When combined with a deep understanding of the customer journey, these elements create a foundation for predictable, scalable growth.

A CRM is more than just a tool—it's a mindset. It's about shifting from a transactional view of business to a relational one. The businesses that succeed in the long term are the ones that invest in relationships, understanding that customers are more than numbers—they are advocates, partners, and, ultimately, the reason we exist. If you have any questions or need help going deeper into your CRM journey, please don't hesitate to reach out to @ mattdeseno on Instagram.

Rethink Everything

CHAPTER 3:

Tag, You're It:
Mastering CRM Organization

INTRODUCTION: BEYOND A ROLODEX

Most businesses today understand that having a CRM (Customer Relationship Management) system is essential. But too often, companies fall into the trap of using their CRM like a glorified digital Rolodex - just a place to store contact information. What they don't realize is that without an effective system to organize and track customer interactions, they're missing out on the real power of a CRM.

That's where tagging comes in. Tagging turns your CRM into a dynamic tool that can segment contacts, trigger automations, and track customer journeys in a meaningful way. Think of tags as labels or markers that allow you to instantly organize, filter, and act on customer data. Whether you're running a simple email campaign or managing complex workflows, tagging is the key to unlocking your CRM's full potential.

While many CRMs offer tagging capabilities, not all tagging systems are created equal. Some can be clunky, overly complex, or poorly integrated. In this chapter, we'll be focusing on HighLevel CRM because it offers a streamlined, intuitive tagging system that makes it easier to organize your contacts, automate processes, and track important customer data. HighLevel's tagging structure is not only more efficient, but it also offers a lower cost of entry and a simpler learning curve compared to other CRMs like HubSpot and SalesForce.

In this chapter, we're going to explore why tagging is so important, how to set up an effective tagging system, and why HighLevel's approach gives you the edge over more expensive, complicated CRMs.

WHAT IS TAGGING IN HIGHLEVEL?

Tagging in HighLevel is like adding little flags to your contacts. These tags help you quickly identify specific details about your customers, track their behaviors, and organize them into meaningful groups. Think of a tag as a label you stick onto a contact so you can instantly filter or act on them later.

For example, if someone books an appointment through your online system, you could assign them a tag like "appt-booked." If they don't show up, you could automatically add the tag "appt-no-show" for easy follow-up. Tagging helps you track actions, behaviors, and characteristics, so you can always stay on top of who your customers are and what they've done.

HighLevel makes tagging easy. You can create tags manually or set up automations that apply tags based on specific actions. The tags are then integrated across your entire system, whether you're running email campaigns, SMS follow-ups, or automated workflows. This means you can instantly filter contacts based on their tags, making it easier to send targeted messages or trigger specific actions.

Tagging isn't just about organization - it's about building smarter, more personalized interactions with your customers. By using tags in HighLevel, you can segment your audience, track customer journeys, and even set up automated processes that respond to customer behavior without you lifting a finger.

TAGGING VS. CUSTOM FIELDS: WHAT'S THE DIFFERENCE?

At first glance, tagging and Custom Fields might seem pretty similar - they both add extra information to a contact. But in reality, they serve different purposes. Understanding when to use tags versus Custom

Fields can make a huge difference in how effectively you organize and automate your CRM.

Tags are like quick labels you apply to contacts to mark actions or characteristics. They're flexible and can be used across different contacts for things like tracking behaviors, segmenting lists, or triggering automations. For example, tags like "sms-opt-in" or "facebook-lead" help you group contacts based on specific actions they've taken. Tags are perfect for organizing contacts into dynamic lists or managing workflows.

On the other hand, **Custom Fields** are more detailed and usually contain specific information unique to a contact. They're not as flexible or universal as tags, but they're great for storing information that's more permanent. For example, a custom field might store a contact's birthday, preferred location, or business size. Custom Fields are often used for personalization within messages, like automatically adding someone's first name to an email, or tracking detailed metrics that don't change frequently.

In short, tags are about **action** and **segmentation**. They help you track what a contact does and how you should interact with them. Custom Fields are about **details**. They hold static information that defines who the contact is. Both are important, but knowing when to use each one ensures you're getting the most out of your CRM.

TAGGING FOR SEGMENTATION

One of the most powerful uses for tags in HighLevel is segmentation. Tagging lets you break your contact list into smaller, more targeted groups based on actions they've taken, characteristics they have, or where they are in the customer journey. This makes it easy to deliver the right message to the right people at the right time.

Segmentation starts with understanding your audience. For example, you might tag contacts based on their **actions**, such as signing up for a newsletter or making a purchase. Tags like "newsletter-opt-in" or "first-purchase" can help you group these contacts and send follow-up messages specifically related to their activity.

You can also segment by **characteristics**, like demographic information or customer preferences. Let's say you have a local business, and you want to target people in specific neighborhoods. You could tag contacts with "location-west-side" or "location-downtown" to deliver personalized offers or promotions based on where they live.

What makes tagging so effective for segmentation is how easily you can create dynamic lists. In HighLevel, once you apply tags, you can instantly filter contacts by any combination of tags and behaviors. This means you're not just creating one-time segments - you're building flexible, evolving groups that update automatically based on what your contacts are doing. Segmentation through tagging lets you personalize your messaging, target specific customer groups, and ultimately create more meaningful interactions. Whether you're running a marketing campaign, following up on leads, or re-engaging past customers, tagging gives you the ability to fine-tune your outreach in a way that feels personal and relevant.

SMART LISTS AND DYNAMIC SEGMENTATION

Tags in HighLevel don't just help you create static groups - they give you the power of **Smart Lists** and **dynamic segmentation**, which automatically update as contacts take actions or meet certain criteria. This is where the true magic of tagging comes into play, because you're not stuck manually organizing your lists over and over again.

A **Smart List** is essentially a saved filter that pulls in contacts based on the tags they've been assigned. Let's say you want to create a list of contacts who have booked an appointment and opted into your SMS list. You can create a Smart List that includes contacts with both "appt-booked" and "sms-opt-in" tags. What makes it dynamic is that as new people book appointments and opt-in, they're automatically added to the list. You never have to lift a finger.

Smart Lists allow you to build and target specific audiences in real time. For example, if you're running a promotion and want to send an email only to people who have downloaded a lead magnet, simply create a Smart List for the "lead-magnet-downloaded" tag. As soon as someone downloads it, they'll be added to that list. This ensures your marketing stays relevant and your lists stay fresh without manual updates.

This dynamic segmentation goes beyond just targeting; it also allows you to exclude certain contacts. You can create lists that filter out specific behaviors. For instance, if someone has already made a purchase, you might exclude them from receiving a promotion for first-time buyers by using a tag like "first-purchase."

Smart Lists and dynamic segmentation take the heavy lifting out of list management, letting you focus on crafting personalized, timely messages. With HighLevel's tagging system, you'll always be in the right place, at the right time, with the right message.

TAGGING IN WORKFLOWS FOR AUTOMATION
Tagging in HighLevel isn't just about organizing your contacts - it plays a critical role in automating your workflows. With the right tags, you can trigger actions, move people through funnels, and even end workflows, all without needing to manually step in. This is where tagging becomes more than just a tool for organization; it becomes a way to streamline your entire customer journey.

Imagine you have a tag like "lead-magnet-downloaded." You can set up a workflow that automatically triggers the moment this tag is applied. Maybe it sends the contact a thank-you email, follows up with additional content, or notifies your sales team to reach out. The contact's action (downloading the lead magnet) applies the tag, and that tag fires off an entire sequence of automated events.

On the flip side, tags can also be used to **end workflows**. Let's say someone books an appointment, and you've been running a sequence of follow-up emails encouraging them to schedule. The moment the tag "appt-booked" is applied, the workflow can stop sending those follow-up emails - because, well, they've already taken the desired action.

In more complex workflows, you might use multiple tags to fine-tune the process. For example, in a chatbot funnel, you could use tags like "ai-chat-started" and "ai-chat-ongoing" to track a contact's progress through the conversation. Depending on which tag is applied, different automation paths can be triggered, allowing the conversation to evolve based on the customer's responses.

By leveraging tags within workflows, you can create a CRM that operates more like a finely-tuned machine. You're not just responding to customer actions - you're predicting them and setting up automations that help move people through their journey in a personalized, efficient way.

TAGGING BEST PRACTICES AND COMMON MISTAKES TO AVOID

Tagging is a powerful tool in HighLevel, but like any tool, it needs to be used properly to be effective. Following best practices can help you keep your CRM clean and organized, while avoiding common mistakes ensures your tags stay useful and efficient.

Use Consistent Naming Conventions

One of the biggest keys to maintaining an organized tagging system is consistency. Stick to a simple naming convention: **all lowercase with hyphens** between words. This keeps your tags readable and uniform across the board. Avoid using spaces, special characters, or inconsistent capitalization. Tags like `source-facebook` are clear and easy to work with, while tags like `Facebook Lead` or `facebook_lead` create unnecessary confusion.

Categorize Your Tags for Clarity

Tags can quickly get out of hand if they're not categorized properly. To avoid this, create distinct categories for your tags. For example:

- Source Tags for where the contact came from (e.g., `source-facebook`, `source-google`).
- Action Tags for tracking behaviors (e.g., `appt-booked`, `sms-opt-in`).
- Campaign Tags for specific marketing efforts (e.g., `holiday-promo`, `spring-sale`).
- Workflow Tags for guiding contacts through

stages (e.g., `ai-chat-started`, `reviews-lead-magnet-sent`).

Categorization makes it easier to search and apply tags without creating too many specific or redundant tags.

Keep Tags Specific, But Not Overly Detailed

It's important to strike a balance between specificity and simplicity. Tags should be descriptive enough to give clear insights but not so detailed that they become hard to manage. Tags like `source-facebook` are useful, but a tag like `source-facebook-ad-campaign-summer-2024` is overly complex and can create clutter. If you need to track more detail, consider using Custom Fields or reports instead of packing everything into tags.

Avoid Over-Tagging

Another common mistake is over-tagging. Adding too many tags to a single contact can lead to confusion and disorganization. If you find yourself adding multiple tags for the same type of action, it's a sign that you may be overdoing it. For example, instead of using separate tags for `first-purchase`, `second-purchase`, and `third-purchase`, a single tag like `purchased` might be more practical.

Failing to Document Your Tags

If you're working with a team - or even just for your own clarity - it's critical to maintain a reference sheet for your tags. Document each tag and its purpose so there's no confusion or overlap. Without documentation, it's easy to accidentally create redundant or conflicting tags, especially as your tagging system grows.

Review and clean up Tags Regularly

Over time, your tag list can become cluttered, especially if you're running multiple campaigns or automations. Make it a habit to review your tags periodically and clean out those that are no longer relevant. This will help keep your tagging system lean, ensuring it remains easy to manage and understand. By following these best practices and avoiding common tagging mistakes, you'll build a CRM system that's well-organized, easy to navigate, and ready to scale as your business grows.

REPORTING AND ANALYTICS USING TAGS

Tags in HighLevel aren't just for organization - they provide powerful insights through reporting and analytics. By using tags strategically, you can track campaign performance, monitor customer journeys, and evaluate the success of automations.

Tracking campaign Performance

Tags help you see which campaigns are performing best. For example, applying a tag like `spring-promo-opt-in` lets you track how many contacts signed up during a specific promotion. By comparing this data to conversions (e.g., with a `purchase-made` tag), you'll know exactly how effective your marketing efforts are.

Monitoring customer Journeys

With tags like `lead-magnet-downloaded` and `appt-booked`, you can follow how leads move through your sales funnel. By identifying where contacts drop off, such as many people downloading your lead magnet but not booking appointments, you can tweak your follow-up strategy to improve conversions.

Analyzing customer Segments

You can easily analyze specific customer segments by tagging contacts from different channels (e.g., `source-facebook` vs. `source-google`) and compare their performance. This data helps you make more informed decisions about where to invest your marketing resources.

Tracking KPIs

Tags offer an easy way to track Key Performance Indicators (KPIs), such as opt-ins, purchases, or no-shows. By pulling reports on tags tied to these actions, you can see how well you're hitting your business goals.

In short, using tags for reporting gives you the data to optimize your marketing, automations, and customer interactions - driving better results for your business.

CONCLUSION:
THE POWER OF AN ORGANIZED CRM

Tags are more than just a way to organize your contacts - they're the backbone of an efficient, scalable CRM system. By using tags in your CRM, you can segment your audience, automate workflows, and track key metrics without the headache of manual sorting or data overload. Whether you're tagging based on actions, customer behaviors, or campaign engagement, the right tagging system transforms your CRM from a static database into a dynamic tool that drives real results.

With a solid tagging strategy - following best practices and avoiding common mistakes - you'll be able to stay on top of customer interactions, streamline processes, and make data-driven decisions with ease. HighLevel's intuitive tagging structure, combined with its automation capabilities, low learning curve, and competitive pricing, makes it an ideal choice for businesses looking to maximize their CRM's potential.

In the end, tagging isn't just about managing contacts - it's about unlocking the full power of your CRM to grow your business smarter and faster.

Rethink Everything

CHAPTER 4:

The Art of Integration: Connecting the Dots

In today's digital age, businesses rely on an ever-growing number of tools to manage functions like sales, marketing, customer support, and more. While each tool serves its purpose, the real challenge is ensuring they work together seamlessly. This chapter explores how a well-integrated Customer Relationship Management (CRM) system can unify these tools, **provide a Single Source of Truth (SSOT)**, and drive efficiency through integrations, AI, and automation. By the end, you'll understand how a CRM can help transform your business into a more well-coordinated, agile operation.

WHY A SINGLE SOURCE OF TRUTH MATTERS

Disconnected systems often lead to confusion and mistakes. For example, your sales team might have one version of a customer's data while your marketing team has another. This fragmentation causes inefficiencies like duplicate efforts, and it can damage customer relationships by providing incorrect or outdated information.

That's not the only issue. Disconnected systems also waste time, and many teams simply don't keep them fully updated because the effort of moving between platforms is too cumbersome. Important updates—like a **critical customer note**—can easily be missed if it's stored in one system while the user is focused on another.

A CRM should act as the **Single Source of Truth (SSOT)** for your business, offering a single, unified view of your customer and business data by integrating information through various methods like **open APIs, webhooks, and built-in integrations**. This ensures seamless data flow across departments. Instead of frequently switching between disconnected tools, all your departments—from marketing to compliance—can access the same, real-time information. This enables teams to collaborate more efficiently, **ensuring that no important information falls through the cracks**. The benefits are clear: increased efficiency, fewer errors, and better decision-making across the board.

THE POWER OF FULL INTEGRATION: BRINGING ALL YOUR TOOLS TOGETHER

From gathering insights from marketing platforms to processing sales with a POS system, a fully integrated CRM forms a unified system, bringing together all the tools you rely on to drive your business. Integrations—whether through **open APIs, webhooks, or other methods**—allow your CRM to unite your data sources, eliminating the need for teams to switch between systems. Instead, they can **access all the information they need in one place**, streamlining workflows and making it easier to get a complete view of the business.

For example, consider a business that previously used separate tools for sales, customer support, and subscription payments. By integrating these systems into a CRM using a variety of methods like **open APIs, webhooks, and built-in connectors**, the company was able to automate monthly billing, track customer interactions in real-time, and provide sales reps up-to-date information when contacting clients. The result? Improved efficiency, fewer missed opportunities, and higher customer satisfaction.

EFFICIENCY THROUGH A SINGLE PANE OF GLASS

Imagine starting your day by logging into your CRM and seeing all your key metrics on one screen: from your marketing performance and lead conversions to sales figures and customer support tickets. This unified view—often referred to as a **"single pane of**

glass"—is the ultimate goal of integration. It provides a dashboard where all relevant data is visible and actionable, helping teams make faster, more informed decisions.

With all your tools connected through your CRM, you avoid the inefficiency of constantly switching between systems. Your team works more efficiently, spotting trends and quickly seizing opportunities in real time. A **single pane of glass** means less time wasted on data gathering and more time focused on strategy and execution.

THE ROLE OF AI IN CRM: AUTOMATING THE MUNDANE AND EMPOWERING YOUR TEAM

Today's CRMs are more than just data repositories. With advancements in Artificial Intelligence (AI), CRMs can now **automate routine tasks and provide powerful insights**. AI handles everything from sending follow-up emails to assigning tasks based on customer behavior, freeing your team from repetitive manual work.

For instance, a CRM with AI capabilities can analyze call interactions between sales reps and clients, score the interaction, detect sentiment, and automate follow-up emails or texts based on the outcome. AI can also suggest the next best steps and update the CRM with relevant statuses in real-time. This saves your team valuable time while helping sales reps act faster, improving customer satisfaction and efficiency. Businesses that incorporate AI into their CRM workflows often see significant increases in performance and customer engagement, as automation frees teams to focus on higher-value tasks.

CUSTOM RULES FOR EVERY DEPARTMENT: TAILORING YOUR CRM

One size doesn't always fit all, especially when it comes to how different teams use a CRM. A robust CRM should offer **custom rules and views tailored to each department's unique requirements**. By providing optimized configurations for every team, a CRM ensures that each department operates efficiently and meets its specific goals.

For example, sales teams may need CRM views focused on closing deals, gathering client details, and tracking leads, while the accounting department may require views centered on payments, subscriptions, and financial data. Additionally, a system that tracks separate statuses for each department can keep records organized without overlap. This means a billing issue can be addressed by accounting, while the support team handles separate client issues—all without missing a beat. Automations can streamline these workflows by triggering follow-up emails, SMS messages, or reminders based on the client's status or interactions.

CONCLUSION:
INTEGRATION IS THE KEY TO BUSINESS SUCCESS

As the digital landscape continues to evolve, the question isn't whether businesses need integration—it's whether they're ready to **unlock the full potential of their tools**. By unifying your systems through a combination of **open APIs, webhooks, and integrations**, you create a Single Source of Truth that eliminates miscommunication, streamlines workflows, and empowers your teams to make informed decisions. When your CRM brings together all your tools and data into a unified system, your business operates more efficiently, adapts to challenges faster, and ultimately delivers a better experience for your customers.

The future of your business starts with **connecting the dots**.

CHAPTER 5:

communication Alchemy: Turning Emails into Dollars

Email schmemail. In a world dominated by fast-moving social media platforms, who cares about the communication strategy of the 90's? However, email remains one of the most **cost-effective and reliable communication tools**—and thanks to advancements in artificial intelligence (AI), creating high-quality email content has never been easier. With the right strategy and tools, email marketing can convert prospects into loyal customers, build engagement, and drive long-term success. Let's dive into the **strategy, metrics, and tools** needed to turn your emails into gold. Whether you're sending newsletters, personal emails, or transactional messages, you'll learn to **alchemize**

your emails into high-converting communication channels.

THE GOLDEN POWER OF EMAIL MARKETING

Though newer digital marketing channels often grab the spotlight, email continues to outperform in **reliability, engagement, and return on investment (ROI).** It's personal, scalable, and **delivers tailored content directly to your audience's inbox.**

Here are some **eye-opening statistics** that showcase the power of email:

- **Email delivers a $36 return for every $1 spent**, making it one of the most profitable marketing channels. But, for many professionals, sending email is FREE! Like, FREE, FREE, FREE.
- **Four billion people** use email worldwide - and it's growing!
- **60% of consumers** say they prefer email as their primary channel for receiving promotional content. This allows the consumer to consume content at their preferred time.
- **Transactional emails**, such as welcome messages or application confirmations, boast open rates between **50% and 60%, far surpassing average marketing campaigns. So, be sure to upsell additional products** in tactical communications where it makes sense.

Beyond these numbers, **email offers a unique ability** to nurture long-term customer relationships. Regular communication builds trust and keeps your brand top-of-mind, ensuring customers **return and recommend you to others.** Also, many people won't remember your name or find your phone number easily. But, a quick search in their email with product terms like "mortgage" or "insurance" can help them find you when needed.

Crafting Newsletters that Engage and Convert

Newsletters are the bread and butter of email marketing. They allow brands to **consistently engage their audience** by sharing valuable content, updates, and promotions. To make your newsletters truly shine, follow these best practices:

Content that Balances Value and Promotion

A winning newsletter contains **a mix of content** that balances educational articles, promotional offers, and, yes, personal updates. Did you recently move, have a child or grandchild, or adopt a new pet? Share it! Keep your audience engaged by offering value, such as tips or insights relevant to their needs. **Overly promotional emails** can drive up unsubscribe rates, so it's essential to maintain this balance.

Consistency is Key

Newsletters build trust when they're delivered **on a predictable schedule.** Whether you send them weekly, bi-weekly, or monthly, consistency helps your audience know when to expect your messages.

A predictable rhythm creates anticipation and familiarity with your brand.

Compelling Subject Lines

Subject lines are the **gatekeepers** to your emails. Research shows that **47% of recipients open emails based solely on subject lines**. A great subject line should be short, relevant, and catchy, hinting at the value inside the email. Personalization, such as using the recipient's name, can also improve open rates.

The best part is that you don't have to spend hours figuring out precisely what to say and how to say it anymore. By harnessing the **power of AI**, you can create personalized, engaging emails. AI tools now generate **compelling subject lines, product recommendations, and content suggestions**, streamlining the email marketing process.

OPTIMIZING EMAIL SIGNATURES: SUBTLE BUT POWERFUL

Many professionals overlook the power of **email signatures**, but this space offers a perfect opportunity to **enhance every communication**. Think of it as a mini marketing tool embedded in every email you send.

Include a Call-to-Action (CTA)

Your email signature can subtly promote **upcoming events, new products, or recent blog posts**. Including a clickable CTA encourages recipients to explore your content without feeling pressured.

Design for Professionalism

A clean, well-organized signature creates a positive impression. Make sure it includes your **name, position, and company logo**. To encourage engagement, you can also link to your social media profiles or website.

Keep It Fresh

Rotate the promotional elements of your signature to **keep it aligned with your latest campaigns**. For example, if you're launching a new product, update your signature to reflect that announcement.

MEASURING SUCCESS: EMAIL KPIS THAT MATTER

You can't manage what you don't measure. Tracking the right Key Performance Indicators (KPIs) ensures you get the most out of your email strategy. Here are the most critical metrics to monitor:

- **Open Rate:** This metric shows the percentage of recipients who opened your email. Depending on your industry, a healthy open rate falls between **15% and 25%.**
- **Click-Through Rate (CTR):** CTR tracks the percentage of recipients who clicked a link within your email. The average CTR is **2-5%**, and higher rates indicate that your content is engaging.

- **Conversion Rate:** This measures how many recipients **completed a desired action**, such as purchasing or filling out a form. The conversion rate is the ultimate indicator of an email's effectiveness.
- **Unsubscribe Rate:** Monitor your unsubscribe rate to **ensure you aren't overwhelming your audience**. A rate below **0.5%** suggests your frequency and content are well-balanced.

Tracking these KPIs allows you to **fine-tune your strategy** and identify what works best for your audience.

CRITICAL: CRM SELECTION & ENGAGEMENT

Selecting a **good Customer Relationship Management (CRM) system** is critical to maximizing the impact of your email strategy. A robust CRM doesn't just store contact information— it **automatically triggers emails based on customer behaviors** (like abandoned carts or special dates), ensuring every message is timely and relevant. It also **tracks engagement metrics**, such as open rates, clicks, and conversions, and **adds these insights to individual customer profiles**. This allows you to build a clearer picture of each contact, precisely segment your audience, and tailor future communications to match their interests and actions.

A well-integrated CRM transforms email marketing from a manual task into **an automated, data-driven powerhouse** that drives meaningful engagement and higher conversion rates.

Turning Your Database into Gold

Stay in touch with your **contacts database** to ensure your audience remains engaged and primed for conversion. **Consistent communication** builds trust and fosters long-term relationships that pay off over time.

- **80% of professionals** say email marketing helps improve customer retention.
- **Segmented campaigns** yield a **760% increase in revenue** by targeting the correct audience with relevant content.
- Customers who receive personalized emails are **5x more likely to become repeat buyers**.

Segment your database to **deliver relevant content to different groups**, such as loyal customers, new leads, or past clients. Also, if you have some clients who only buy life insurance from you and others who only purchase an auto, design different messaging for each and try cross-selling your portfolio. **Tailoring your message** ensures your emails feel personalized and valuable, increasing the chances of conversion.

CONCLUSION:
ALCHEMIZE YOUR EMAIL STRATEGY

Your email database is gold waiting to be mined—start digging by crafting thoughtful, consistent, and engaging emails. With every message, you build trust, foster loyalty, and nurture long-term relationships that drive business growth. You can't stay in front of all your customers all the time, but your technology can.

CHAPTER 6:

Beyond the Inbox:
Multichannel CRM communication

Email has long been the cornerstone of customer communication, but it's no longer enough in today's digital age. Customers are increasingly active across multiple channels, from social media to instant messaging and texting. To effectively engage with your audience, it's essential to adopt a multichannel communication strategy that meets them where they are.

THE EMAIL ERA:
STILL RELEVANT, BUT NOT SUFFICIENT

While email remains a powerful tool, it's essential to recognize its limitations. Inboxes are often overcrowded, spam filters are becoming more sophisticated, and customers' attention spans are shrinking. You need to supplement email with other communication channels to ensure your messages are seen and heard.

SMS: A DIRECT AND POWERFUL CHANNEL

SMS, or text messaging, offers a highly effective way to reach customers directly and immediately. With open rates significantly higher than email, SMS can be used for time-sensitive promotions, appointment reminders, service alerts, and urgent updates. However, it's crucial to use SMS judiciously and only send messages to customers who have opted in to receive them.

INSTANT MESSAGING: REAL-TIME ENGAGEMENT

Instant messaging platforms like WhatsApp, Facebook Messenger, and Slack provide a more conversational and interactive way to communicate with customers. They offer real-time engagement, allowing you to quickly address questions, resolve issues, and provide personalized support. Integrating instant messaging into your CRM can streamline your communication efforts and enhance customer satisfaction.

SOCIAL MEDIA: ENGAGING WITH YOUR AUDIENCE

Social media platforms have become essential for

customer engagement. By integrating social media into your CRM, you can:

- **Schedule posts:** Plan and publish content across multiple platforms to maintain a consistent presence.
- **Monitor conversations:** Track mentions of your brand and respond promptly to customer inquiries.
- **Build community:** Foster a sense of community around your brand by encouraging interactions and engaging with your audience.

THE POWER OF MULTICHANNEL INTEGRATION

To truly maximize the effectiveness of your communication strategy, it's essential to integrate multiple channels into your CRM system. This allows you to:

- **Create a unified customer view:** Track all customer interactions across different channels to comprehensively understand their needs and preferences.
- **Deliver consistent experiences:** Ensure your messaging and branding are consistent across all channels, reinforcing your brand identity.
- **Automate workflows:** Send follow-up emails after a customer engages on social media to automate repetitive tasks and improve efficiency.

CRAFTING A SUCCESSFUL MULTICHANNEL STRATEGY

To effectively implement a multichannel communication strategy, consider the following:

- **Understand your customers' preferences:** Identify the channels your customers most frequently use and tailor your messaging accordingly.
- **Use automation wisely:** Leverage automation to streamline repetitive tasks and improve efficiency, but avoid overwhelming customers with excessive messages.
- **Maintain consistency:** Ensure your messaging and branding are consistent across all channels.
- **Track and analyze results:** Monitor the performance of your multichannel communication efforts and make adjustments as needed.

BEYOND THE BASICS: ADVANCED MULTICHANNEL TACTICS

In addition to the core principles outlined above, consider these advanced strategies to enhance your multichannel communication further:

- **Personalization:** Utilize AI-powered tools to personalize messages based on customer data and preferences.

- **Omnichannel journeys:** Map out customer journeys across multiple channels to ensure a seamless experience.
- **Measure and optimize:** Use analytics to track your multichannel campaigns' performance and identify improvement areas.
- **Stay updated on trends:** Stay ahead with emerging communication channels and technologies.

CONCLUSION

The future of customer communication is multichannel. By integrating multiple channels into your CRM strategy, you can enhance customer engagement, improve satisfaction, and drive business growth. By understanding your customers' preferences, utilizing automation, maintaining consistency, and tracking results, you can create a personalized and effective multichannel communication experience that sets your business apart.

Rethink Everything

CHAPTER 7:

Supercharge Your CRM: Unlocking Hidden Powers

Ever feel like your CRM is just sitting there, not pulling its weight? Ready to transform it from another tool into your business's secret weapon? Let's talk about bringing artificial intelligence into the mix.

AI is everywhere nowadays—it's the buzzword on everyone's lips. Remember when the internet became a big deal in the late '90s and early 2000s? AI is having that kind of moment right now. So why let your CRM miss all the cool tricks AI brings? Your CRM is already smart, but we can crank it up to genius level with AI.

As a small business owner, you're juggling a million things—marketing, sales, customer service, you name it. It can get pretty overwhelming. But what if your CRM could lighten the load and become your smartest assistant? You can turn your CRM into a powerhouse without needing a huge budget or a tech degree by tapping into features like lead scoring, AI-driven messaging, and chatbots.

Let's dive into some practical steps to unlock these hidden powers in your CRM, making your life easier and your customers happier.

#1
LEAD SCORING:
REDICTING YOUR NEXT CUSTOMER

Imagine if you could tell which customers are most likely to buy from you next. Lead scoring does that—it helps you focus on the folks who are most interested in what you offer.

Most CRMs on the market today have a form of Lead Scoring. It's usually under something like "Opportunities" or "Leads." Consider actions showing a customer is interested and assign points to each action. For example, you might add points when someone visits your website, opens an email, clicks a link, fills out a form, interacts on social media, or purchases a product.

Use your CRM's automation features to update these scores automatically. Set up triggers so that their score goes up whenever a customer does one of these actions. Create a list or dashboard that shows you who has the highest scores. These are your hot leads—the people you should contact first.

Let's say you run an online boutique. A customer signs up for your newsletter, opens your welcome email, and clicks on a product link. As they keep interacting with your business, their score climbs, signaling they're ready for a special offer or a personal touch.

#2
USING AI FOR PERSONALIZED MESSAGING

We all love getting messages that feel like they were written just for us. AI can help you send personalized messages that resonate with your customers.

Check your CRM settings and enable any available AI or intelligent features. Use AI to help write email subject lines and content. You can input prompts like, "Write a friendly follow-up email for someone who just attended our webinar." If these features aren't available in your CRM, you can use a free version of ChatGPT to help you.

Include the customer's name and reference their specific actions or interests. Segment your audience so you're sending the right message to the right people. Schedule emails or texts to go out automatically based on certain triggers, like when a lead reaches a specific score or completes an action.

If you offer fitness coaching and someone downloads your free workout guide, your AI can automatically send them a personalized email thanking them and offering a discount on your coaching services.

#3
SETTING UP AN AI CHATBOT AS YOUR CUSTOMER SERVICE ASSISTANT

Imagine having a customer service rep who works 24/7 without a paycheck. That's basically what an AI chatbot can do for you.

Start by finding the chatbot or live chat feature in your CRM. Customize it to match your brand with your colors and a friendly greeting. Think about the questions you get and program the answers into your chatbot.

For example, when someone asks, "What are your store hours?" the chatbot can reply, "We're open Monday through Friday, 9 AM to 5 PM." If they ask about shipping, it can tell them, "Yes, we offer free shipping on orders over $50!"

You can train your chatbot to handle more complex inquiries by uploading product information, detailed FAQs, and even transcripts from your company's sales or customer service calls. This will make your chatbot more thoughtful and helpful.

But let's take a step further. Adding your customer reviews and transcripts from past interactions lets your chatbot pick up on the language and solutions your team typically provides. This means it can handle questions in a way that feels personal and consistent with your brand's voice.

Upload your menu, product info, or FAQs so the chatbot can handle more complex inquiries. Test it out to make sure it's working properly, then deploy it on your website and monitor its performance. Tweak as necessary.

Say you own a local pizza restaurant. Late at night, customers might visit your site with questions like, "Do you have a gluten-free option?" Your chatbot can answer immediately, "Yes, we offer a delicious gluten-free crust for our medium and large pizzas! Would you like to place an order or see our gluten-free menu?"

Remember, your chatbot is an extension of your customer service team. The more effort you put into training it with your company's specific knowledge, the more effective it will be in assisting your customers. Just like hiring a new employee who knows nothing about your business, you must train them to understand all aspects of your operations. The difference is that with the chatbot, you only have to tell it once, and it will remember everything, ideally forever. It won't guess or misinterpret information the way humans might.

It's like having a super-employee who's always on duty, helping to improve customer satisfaction and boost sales.

#4
AUTOMATING FOLLOW-UPS BASED ON LEAD SCORES

Following up with potential customers is critical, but it can be time-consuming. Automate it!

Set up a workflow in your CRM that kicks in when a lead reaches a specific score. Decide what lead score will trigger an action, such as when a lead hits 25 points.

Define what happens next. You might send them a personalized email with a special offer, assign them to a team member for a follow-up call, or update their status in your CRM. Use conditions to customize the follow-up based on specific factors like what product they're interested in. Once everything's set up, turn it on and let your CRM do the work.

After interacting with your content, a lead reaches 30 points. Your CRM automatically sends them a discount code and alerts you to give them a call so you can engage with them at just the right time.

#5
MEASURING SUCCESS AND
TWEAKING YOUR STRATEGY

You can't improve what you don't measure. Monitor your progress and make adjustments as needed.

Regularly check email open rates, click-through rates, and conversion rates. Evaluate your lead scoring—is it accurately identifying hot leads? If not, adjust how you assign points.

Test different versions of your emails or chatbot responses to see what works best. Review the chatbot logs to see any questions it couldn't answer and update accordingly. Ask your customers how you're doing. Their insights can help you improve.

You notice that emails sent on Wednesdays get opened more often. Adjust your schedule to send emails on that day. If your chatbot gets a specific question, ensure it knows the answer.

CONCLUSION

Your CRM doesn't have to be just another piece of software—it can be the MVP of your business tools. By adding AI into the mix, you're turning it into a supercharged assistant that helps you work smarter, not harder.

I predict that AI will significantly impact CRMs in the near future, making them easier to use and simplifying the process of analyzing data to predict what to do next or suggest ways to improve. Don't let your CRM miss out on the benefits AI offers. Log in today and start exploring these features. Begin with something simple like setting up lead scoring or creating a basic chatbot. Keep an eye on the results and tweak your strategies as you go. Every little step brings you closer to a more efficient and profitable business.

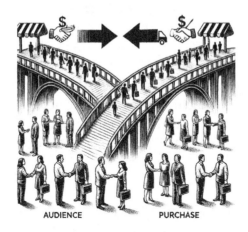

AUDIENCE   PURCHASE

CHAPTER 8:

crafting the Perfect call to Action: The cRM Magnet

WHY THE CALL TO ACTION IS A MARKETING FUNDAMENTAL

A call to action (CTA) is one of the most critical elements in any online marketing strategy. It's not just a button or a simple link; it's the bridge between your audience and the action that leads them to conversion. When done right, a CTA can transform your traffic into leads, your leads into customers, and your customers into long-term advocates. The CTA is a single variable that has driven billions in online sales, and it is often the fastest way to increase conversions without driving more traffic.

Imagine this: You drive 1,000 visitors to your landing page, and your CTA converts at 1%. That gives you ten leads. What if you could tweak your CTA to convert at 2%? That simple change just doubled your leads without any extra traffic. This is the power of the CTA. For many businesses, the success or failure of their website—and their entire marketing efforts— rests mainly on the performance of their calls to action.

THE FOUNDATIONS OF EVERY CTA

In every marketing campaign, three essential components lead to revenue: traffic, a landing page, and a call to action. You can generate all the traffic in the world and build the most visually stunning landing pages, but if your CTA isn't compelling enough, you're leaving money on the table.

A high-quality CTA doesn't happen by accident. It is designed with intention, with the buyer's journey in mind, and with careful consideration of placement, copy, and timing. Here are some key points to focus on:

CTA Placement, color, and Quantity

The placement of your CTA can make or break its effectiveness. Above the fold, clear, and in a contrasting color that draws attention are basics but often overlooked. Make sure your CTA isn't just tucked away at the bottom of the page. A good rule of thumb is that if a user has to hunt for it, it's already lost. You also want to be cautious of overwhelming users with too many CTAs. Balance is key.

CTA Diversity

Every visitor to your site isn't at the same stage in the buying process. You need to cater to various stages of the customer journey. For example, someone at the research stage might respond to a CTA for a free resource like a case study or guide. Someone further down the funnel may be more interested in scheduling a demo. Current customers might need an upsell or a limited-time discount. CTA diversity is crucial for capturing leads no matter where they are in their journey.

CTA Urgency

Emphasize urgency in a realistic way that aligns with your audience's needs. The proper sense of urgency can push visitors to act immediately, but it must be believable. For example, one client in the beauty and Cryoskin industry had ads converting at just 3%. Their original CTA, "57% off Cryoskin," lacked a time-sensitive offer and was buried at the bottom of the page. By adjusting the CTA to "50% off Your 1st Cryo Session" and adding a clear deadline of "valid through Dec. 15th," the conversion rate skyrocketed to over 20% within 30 days. This shows the impact of urgency done right.

Urgency should feel natural, not forced. Overdoing it with false scarcity or exaggerated time limits can lead to mistrust. Keep it authentic to the situation, offering solutions with a clear benefit tied to acting sooner rather than later. Whether offering a limited-time discount or highlighting availability, urgency can make all the difference when implemented thoughtfully and in a way that resonates with your audience's immediate needs.

CTA Button Copy

What the button says matters. Generic phrases like "Submit" or "Contact Us" won't cut it. Use action-driven language that tells visitors exactly what they'll get, increasing the perceived value. Think about the visitor's psychology—what problems have led them to your page, and how can you help solve them? Instead of "Learn More," try something specific, like "Get Your Free Marketing Report in 5 Minutes."

COMMON CALL TO ACTION MISTAKES: WHAT TO AVOID

CTAs, when crafted poorly, can sink an otherwise well-executed campaign. Here are some common mistakes that can drastically reduce the effectiveness of your CTAs:

Low Perceived Value

A CTA like "Contact Us" often leads to low conversion rates because it offers no real value upfront. Don't rely on user initiative—always provide value first. When crafting your CTA, ask yourself, "What is the immediate value for the visitor?"

High Perceived Risk

When potential leads perceive too much risk or

unknowns, they won't click. This applies across industries, whether SaaS, e-commerce, or service-based businesses. Is it unclear what they will receive? Are there hidden costs? Are you missing critical details like reviews, office hours, or shipping information? Remove as much uncertainty as possible. By answering fundamental questions upfront, you lower the perceived risk and encourage conversions.

CTA Placement

Burying your CTA at the bottom of the page or in places where it doesn't make sense is a surefire way to hurt conversion rates. Consider the intent of each CTA based on where it is placed on your site. For example, an upsell CTA should be on the product page, not above the fold on the homepage.

Disconnected from the Sales Process

Your CTA should seamlessly connect with your sales process. If there's a disconnect, it can lead to poor-quality leads and lower close rates. For example, your lead will feel misled if your CTA offers a "Free Quote" and the sales rep immediately pitches an unrelated service. Your sales team must understand what each CTA promises and follow through consistently.

When it comes to common CTA mistakes, I often see a disconnect between the CTA and the sales process. Your sales process must align with what the prospect expects from the CTA. One encounter involved a marketing agency whose CTA promised a "Free Marketing Report." Instead of delivering the report upfront, their sales reps would call leads and try to sell SEO services first, only sending the report afterward. Despite cycling through multiple sales reps, their close rates remained stagnant. I recommended they reverse the order and present the marketing report before attempting to sell anything. By delivering value upfront, they saw a steady increase in close rates for six consecutive months. Prospects got precisely what they expected from the CTA, and once their initial expectations were met, they were much more willing to make a purchase.

The best way to avoid this disconnect is to define your sales process before creating the CTA. This can streamline your process and enhance the value of your CTAs. For instance, if your sales process often involves a live demo, consider creating a universal demo video that your CTA can lead to. After the first minute, you can request the prospect's email to continue. This approach keeps the process efficient and provides value early, ensuring the CTA and sales strategy flow together seamlessly.

WRITING A HIGH-VALUE CALL TO ACTION

Think of your call to action as a lifeline. Imagine your audience is in a bad situation—say they just received a flash flood warning to evacuate, and you're offering the only bus out. The first words out of your mouth must be clear, compelling, and complete with trust. What would you say? "Bring your family, pets, and one bag each. We're headed to safety at XYZ. No cost to you."

That's the level of clarity and urgency your CTAs need. Replace the flood with a business problem; your CTA is the bus to safety. What would make someone take action? Clarity and trust.

HOW TO WRITE A WINNING CTA

Increase Perceived Value

Offer more than just the basics. If your CTA is to schedule a demo, add something irresistible like "Schedule your Free Demo & Get a Custom Marketing Plan." The more value they perceive, the more likely they'll convert.

Reduce Perceived Risks

Provide clear context around your CTA to eliminate uncertainties. Include customer reviews, testimonials, guarantees, or clear explanations about pricing. People need to know exactly what they're getting and why they should trust you.

Prominent Placement

Use bold, contrasting colors, and make your CTA easy to find on every page. Make sure the copy stands out and is action-oriented. Don't just say "Learn More"—use language like "Download the Free Guide Now" or "Start Your 14-Day Free Trial."

Align with the Sales Process

Ensure your CTA aligns perfectly with your sales funnel. If your CTAs change, keep your sales team or anyone talking to leads up-to-date. The more in sync your CTAs are with the sales process, the higher your close rates will be.

USING TEMPLATES FOR SCALABILITY AND PREDICTABLE RESULTS

When I say "templates," I'm not talking about cookie-cutter, one-size-fits-all approaches. In GoHighLevel, templates are about creating niche-specific, data-driven pages that are custom-made to generate results. These templates aren't just pretty—they're functional, built, and tested for conversion.

The beauty of GoHighLevel is how easily you can build and split-test the CTAs of your templates. Once you find a winning CTA, you can update your snapshot templates to scale and improve performance across your clients.

Templates aren't just about speed but consistency and proven results. A well designed template can be customized for any client, allowing you to deliver results faster and with predictable outcomes. Incorporating proven templates into your GoHighLevel offers enhances the effectiveness of each CTA, adding value and making them more compelling to your audience.

THE 1-2 PUNCH: COMBINING TEMPLATES WITH THE RIGHT CTA

Crafting a perfect call to action is about understanding

your audience's needs, reducing their perceived risk, and offering them an irresistible value proposition. Whether you're testing different colors, placements, or CTA copy, your ultimate goal is to get people to take action and move through the sales process seamlessly.

By leveraging templates in GoHighLevel, you can scale these efforts across multiple clients, providing consistent, high-quality results. With the right CTAs and proven templates, you're not just improving conversion rates but building long-term, scalable success.

Keep refining. Keep testing. And always remember, the perfect CTA paired with a proven template can be your CRM magnet for years to come.

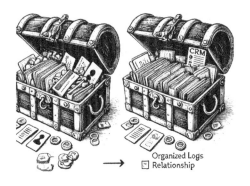

Organized Logs
☑ Relationship

CHAPTER 9:

Data Treasures:
Unearthing CRM Gold Mines

In the vast landscape of sales and marketing, the quest for more leads, more contacts, and, ultimately, more business often leads professionals down a path where quantity overshadows quality. The allure of a massive database—thousands upon thousands of contacts—promises endless opportunities. But what if this approach is more fool's gold than treasure? What if the true gold mine lies not in the expanse of your data but in the depth of your relationships?

THE MISCONCEPTION OF "MORE"

The common misconception among sales professionals is that a more extensive database equals more business. Agents proudly boast about databases with 20,000 or even 30,000 contacts, believing that sheer numbers will drive success. However, the reality is starkly different. According to industry observations, over 64% of agents don't have any database, and among those who do, many struggle to manage it effectively.

An enormous list of contacts is not inherently valuable if you can't maintain meaningful relationships with those on it. The "R" in CRM stands for "Relationship," which transforms a static list of names into a dynamic tool for business growth.

DATABASE VS. CRM: UNDERSTANDING THE DIFFERENCE

It's crucial to distinguish between a database and a Customer Relationship Management (CRM) system. A database is a collection of contacts—names, phone numbers, email addresses—often stored in a spreadsheet or a box of business cards. It's one-dimensional and lacks the interactive components that foster relationships.

On the other hand, a CRM is a multi-dimensional platform designed to manage interactions with current and potential customers. It tracks communication history, schedules follow-ups, and provides insights that help deepen relationships. It's not a one-time task to check off your to-do list; it's an ongoing process that evolves as your relationships grow.

THE FALLACY OF VANITY METRICS

In an age where social media likes, shares, and impressions are often touted as measures of success, it's easy to get sidetracked by vanity metrics. Marketing teams might celebrate a post that receives 150 likes, but if none of those engagements translate into sales, what's the real value?

Focusing on these superficial numbers can paralyze efforts and distract from what truly matters—converting relationships into revenue. Instead of chasing likes, professionals should concentrate on metrics that directly impact their bottom line.

SIMPLIFYING TRACKING
FOR MAXIMUM IMPACT

Overcomplicating tracking systems can be just as detrimental as not tracking at all. The key is to make tracking simple yet effective. For instance, implementing a strategy to send two personalized postcards and make a follow-up phone call can be more impactful than a complex campaign lacking a personal touch.

The goal is to create touchpoints that add value and foster genuine connections. By simplifying your tracking methods, you can easily stay consistent and measure what truly works.

THE POWER OF PERSONAL CONNECTIONS

In the early days of my career, I learned the immense value of personal connections. I recall reaching out to every award-winning agent I could find simply to learn from them. Surprisingly, every single one was willing to talk to me. This experience reinforced the idea that people are generally open to genuine interactions.

Building relationships through storytelling and shared experiences creates a strong foundation for trust. Social media platforms offer unprecedented opportunities to engage with clients personally. Instead of using these platforms solely to broadcast messages, we can use them to listen, engage, and better understand our clients.

QUALITY OVER QUANTITY: THE 100-PERSON PRINCIPLE

Imagine focusing your efforts on a carefully curated list of 100 contacts. If nurtured properly, these relationships could generate $100,000 in gross commission income (GCI). By doubling the list to 200, you might double your GCI. The principle is that a smaller, well-managed list can be far more lucrative than an unwieldy database of thousands.

This approach allows for more meaningful interactions. You can remember birthdays, celebrate anniversaries, understand personal interests, and strengthen the client-agent bond.

UTILIZING TECHNOLOGY
TO ENHANCE RELATIONSHIPS

Technology should be a tool to enhance relationships, not replace them. A CRM system can remind you of important dates, log interactions, and help segment your contacts for targeted communication. But the system is only as good as your effort to use it effectively.

For example, instead of sending generic messages, use your CRM to note fun facts about your clients—their favorite sports teams, hobbies, or recent life events. This information lets you personalize your communications, making each interaction more meaningful.

THE ART OF ADDING VALUE

Every touchpoint with a client should add value. A mass email reminding clients to turn back their clocks for daylight saving time is unlikely to impress anyone. Instead, consider what information or assistance would genuinely benefit them.

Perhaps you could provide a personalized market analysis of their neighborhood, offer insights into home maintenance tips for the upcoming season, or share exclusive opportunities relevant to their interests. The goal is to be seen as a salesperson and a trusted advisor.

REAL-LIFE APPLICATION:
THE BIRTHDAY LUNCH STRATEGY

A simple yet effective strategy I've employed involves turning social media interactions into real-world connections. When friends and clients wish me a happy birthday on Facebook, I respond with a personalized video message thanking them and inviting them to lunch.

This approach led to 45 days of lunch meetings, each an opportunity to strengthen relationships and discuss potential business opportunities. Not only did this generate new leads, but it also reinforced existing connections—all while enjoying good company and conversation.

AVOIDING THE ONE-NIGHT STAND MENTALITY

One of the pitfalls in sales is treating clients like one-night stands—focusing solely on closing the deal and moving on. This short-term mindset overlooks the long-term value of client relationships. An impactful anecdote comes from a client who, upon closing, said, "I suppose I won't see you anymore because you got your check."

This was a wake-up call. It highlighted the importance of continuing the relationship beyond the transaction. By staying engaged with clients after the sale, you position yourself as their go-to professional for future needs and referrals.

EMBRACING THE RELATIONSHIP-FOCUSED CRM

The essence of a successful CRM strategy lies in embracing the relationship component. It's about consistent, meaningful interactions rather than sporadic, impersonal communications. Here are some actionable steps to implement this approach:

- **Curate Your Contact List:** Focus on clients who align with your business values and will likely generate referrals.
- **Personalize Communications:** Use your CRM to track personal details and customize your messages accordingly.
- **Add Genuine Value:** Ensure every interaction offers something beneficial to the client.
- **Leverage Technology Wisely:** Utilize CRM features to stay organized, but don't rely on automation to build relationships.
- **Track Meaningful Metrics:** Focus on conversions, referrals, and client retention rather than vanity metrics like likes and impressions.

CONCLUSION

To unearth the gold mines within our CRMs, we must shift our focus from accumulating vast amounts of data to cultivating rich relationships. We transform our CRM from a static database into a dynamic tool for sustainable growth by simplifying tracking, personalizing our interactions, and consistently adding value.

Remember, the true treasures in your CRM are not the number of contacts but the depth of your connections. Nurture them well, and they will yield rewards far beyond the initial transaction.

CHAPTER 10:

Reports that Matter:
Turning Numbers into Narratives

"If you don't know your numbers, you don't know your business."

Calvin Mergen Reports That Matter: Turning Numbers into Narratives

The data or numbers derived from your CRM directly reflect your business's narrative. Whether you're managing a real estate team, working as a lender, or running a small or large company focused on sales, the reports pulled from your CRM (Customer Relationship Management system) offer more than a snapshot of operations - they tell the story of where your business has been, where your business currently is and where it's heading in the future. In today's fast-paced and ever-changing markets, using this data to fuel decision-making is no longer optional; it's critical. The key is understanding which numbers matter and how to turn them into a narrative that drives internal growth and fuels external marketing efforts.

UNDERSTANDING THE RIGHT DATA: THE BACKBONE OF YOUR BUSINESS

CRMs capture vast amounts of information, but not all data points are equally important. Identifying which numbers to focus on can mean the difference between reacting to daily chaos and driving your business toward strategic goals.

Lead Management and conversion Data

The lead management process and its systems are at the heart of any successful business. This starts with knowing how many leads are coming into your system and where they are coming from. The leads generated represent your marketing effectiveness, whether those leads come from referrals, social media, or your website.

Tracking lead sources aids in determining which marketing channels are working the best. Are most of your leads coming from organic search or paid ads? Perhaps your email marketing campaign is driving the majority of new business. Or is your repeat and referral business through the roof? Knowing this allows you to allocate resources efficiently, ensuring your marketing spend is focused on the most lucrative channels.

Of equal importance is conversion data—how many of those leads are turning into actual dollars. The conversion rate measures the effectiveness of your sales and nurturing processes. A high conversion rate indicates that your team is doing something right. On the flip side, a low conversion rate points to potential issues.

Action Item: Ensure that your sources and tags are accurate and allow easy data extraction from your CRM. This makes reporting and marketing so much easier in the long run. Consider a sub-source as well. For example, the lead you are tracking initially came from your sphere of influence, yet you also want to know what prompted them to start a conversation TODAY. That could be a newsletter, postcard, phone call, social media post, event, etc. This allows for an even deeper understanding of how to spend your lead generation and marketing dollars.

Pipeline and Deal Tracking

The sales pipeline is your business's roadmap. CRM data shows not only the number of deals in the pipeline but also each deal's stage, allowing you to forecast revenue and identify stalling deals.

Pipeline reports help you prioritize your efforts. For example, if most of your deals are stuck in the negotiation stage, it may indicate that your team needs better negotiation tools or a pricing issue. On the other hand, if deals get to the contract stage and then fall through, it could point to a breakdown in client communications or operational inefficiencies.

A key element of deal tracking is understanding deal velocity - how long it takes for a lead to move through the pipeline. Faster deal cycles often correlate with smooth operations and strong client engagement, while longer cycles could mean inefficiencies that must be addressed.

Action Item: Track pipeline stages in your CRM. If your CRM does not offer "stage" tracking, create tags, color coding, or utilize an available tool to ensure you can quickly identify those in a particular stage. You may want to start a separate spreadsheet for this tracking. Commitment to Excellence (CTE) is an excellent tool for pipeline tracking. The more you know your numbers, the better you will know what activities to focus on to reach goals.

Client Relationship Management

In sales, relationships are everything! CRM systems track every client interaction, from phone calls to in-person meetings. These records provide a window into client engagement and satisfaction. The more consistently you engage with your clients, the stronger your relationships will be.

High-value CRM data includes client activity and engagement metrics, such as the frequency of interactions and touchpoints (calls, emails, texts, etc.). Use this information to tailor communications to specific clients, ensuring that their needs are being met proactively rather than reactively.

Tracking repeat clients and referrals is another vital piece of the puzzle. Suppose your CRM shows that many businesses come from repeat customers or referrals. In that case, it strongly indicates that your customer service and client relationship strategies are working. This is particularly valuable in industries where trust and long-term relationships are paramount.

Action Item: Determine if your CRM has a mobile app. If so, use it! Track every interaction in your CRM, even if your CRM does not make the interaction. Vital data such as this needs to be in a centralized location. Enlist systems such as Seven Levels of Communication or Touch Plans to streamline communication and automate wherever possible.

Marketing Performance Data

Having a CRM that tracks your marketing campaigns' effectiveness is crucial. Metrics like email open rates, click-through rates, and campaign ROI (return on investment) are invaluable for gauging which strategies resonate with your audience.

By tracking marketing performance, you can refine your messaging and adjust the timing of your outreach, continuously improving your engagement tactics.

Action Item: Set up A/B testing in your CRM or via spreadsheet. Analyze these reports after each campaign to implement data-driven improvements for future efforts.

Revenue, Return on Investment and Financial Metrics

While CRM data helps you understand client behavior and engagement, it also plays a crucial role in tracking financial performance. Data like return on investment per client, total closed deal value, and forecasted revenue help you understand the monetary impact of your CRM efforts.

Knowing how much return on investment each client generates allows you to prioritize high-value relationships and decide where to focus resources, leading to better goal planning. ROI-related CRM data provides a snapshot of your current performance and helps you anticipate future trends. By analyzing past revenue patterns, you can set realistic yet ambitious growth targets for the months and years ahead.

Action Item: Track ROI on lead sources and sub-sources. Pull monthly reports to ensure lead generation dollars are being spent effectively. If your CRM lacks robust tracking, use tools like CTE for real-time financial metrics.

Operational Efficiency Metrics

In addition to tracking deals and revenue, a CRM is an excellent tool for improving operational efficiency. Task and activity completion rates provide insight into how well your team manages their workload. Are tasks being completed on time, or are there bottlenecks in the process?

Similarly, tracking time to close - how long it takes for a deal to move from prospect to completion helps identify where delays occur. If deals are stalling at the contract or final negotiation stages, it could be a sign that the process, people, or vendors might need to be adjusted.

Action Item: Seeing is believing. Choose a CRM that allows for transaction management and task tracking. This will illuminate allied resources that potentially need to be changed, staff that need to be upgraded, and systems that need to be improved.

Client Segmentation and Demographics

Knowing your clients on a deeper level is essential for tailoring your messaging and services. CRM systems allow you to segment clients based on buyer vs. seller, budget range, or geographic location. This segmentation enables more personalized services, increasing the likelihood of conversion.

For example, by segmenting clients based on geographic location, you can customize marketing materials to reflect local market trends, increasing relevance, market share, and engagement. Segmentation also allows you to identify untapped markets or areas where your business could expand.

Action item: Tracking zip codes through tags and quickly pulling that report tells your business's market share story. It is not necessary for everyone, yet it is essential to your company and tells your story. This information is vital for targeted marketing efforts.

TURNING DATA INTO A BUSINESS NARRATIVE

Data without context is just noise. The real power of CRM data lies in turning it into a narrative that informs both your internal strategies and external marketing. For instance, if your pipeline data shows that deals in a specific neighborhood are closing faster than others, you can use that story to adjust your marketing message, positioning yourself as the go-to expert.

Marketing becomes more effective when backed by data-driven insights. Instead of generic marketing, your business narrative becomes one of success stories and evidence-based strategies. When you share these stories with clients - whether in a social media post, a listing presentation, or a newsletter - you position yourself as a data-driven professional grounded in results.

A CRM is not just a tool for tracking deals and clients but for crafting your business's story. The numbers you track are the threads that, when woven together, create a comprehensive narrative of growth, success, and opportunity. Understanding which data points matter most and turning those numbers into actionable insights can elevate your business internally and in your client's eyes. Your CRM doesn't just reflect where your business is; it shows where it's going, which is the story worth telling!

CHAPTER 11:

unlocking the Hidden Gold in Your CRM: Your Guide to Email Marketing Mastery

Your best leads are already in your CRM.

These people have already met you, engaged with you, or shown interest in your mortgage services. They're closer to making a decision. Unlike people surfing the internet or asking for referrals from a real estate agent, the leads in your CRM have taken the first few steps toward closing a deal.

People in your CRM are either inbound leads (who've inquired with you) or outbound leads (you've already shared your value proposition with them). These are your highest-probability leads.

117

New leads, while valuable, represent fresh opportunities but often come with a lower probability of converting. Don't fall into the trap of thinking new leads are always your best.

So, how do we move these CRM leads forward at scale?

Email marketing–in this context, I call it email outreach.

My goal for this chapter is simple: help you turn leads into clients and build a steady flow of new leads through referrals and repeat customers. What you're about to read isn't theory—it's the system I've built and tested as a mortgage broker and a service to my clients. It's responsible for generating over a million dollars in new revenue annually.

The best part? It's not complicated. You likely already have everything you need to convert leads in your CRM. You don't have to be a marketing expert; you just need to start a conversation and say what you know.

Let's dive in and get some easy wins.

STEP 1
Keep It Simple—Send Two Emails a week

You don't need to bombard your leads with daily emails, but you don't want them to forget you. According to HubSpot, sending two weekly emails strikes the right balance (HubSpot Blog).

Try This Today:
- **Mid-week Email:** Focus on education. For example, "3 Ways to Improve Your Credit Score Before Applying for a Mortgage" or "How to Choose the Best Mortgage for Your Situation."
- **Weekend Email:** Offer something actionable but low-pressure, like "Lock in Your Mortgage Rate This Week" or "Get a Free Rate Check Before Monday."

Pro Tip: If your open and unsubscribe rates remain steady, experiment with a third email when something timely happens—like significant rate movements or changes in market conditions. Leverage events that affect your leads and offer them relevant advice when they need it most.

STEP 2
Segment Your Leads—Even with a Small List

I don't think segmentation is just for big companies. You can segment a small list to target leads based on their position in the mortgage process. Research by Mailchimp shows that segmented email campaigns have 14.31% higher open rates (Mailchimp).

Try This Today:
Create three primary segments:
- **New Leads:** Educate them about mortgage options and why they should choose you.
- **Hot Leads:** They've shown interest—now give them the extra nudge to convert, like

offering a free consultation or quote.
- **Existing Clients:** These are your referral goldmines. Keep them engaged with market updates and referral incentives.

Pro Tip: Don't rely on spreadsheets. Most CRMs make it easy to segment leads automatically based on their status. Leveraging your CRM is critical to avoiding missed opportunities and scaling your sales production.

STEP 3
Make Your Emails Mobile-Friendly

Over 80% of users check their emails on mobile devices. Your emails must look clean and professional on the phone. The good news? This makes your job easier—simple text-based emails often perform the best—no need for fancy designs or images.

Try This Today:
When emailing mortgage leads:
- **Keep it short:** Aim for under 100 words.
- **Use one strong CTA**, like "Review Your Refinance Options."
- **Consider scheduling links:** We're seeing these gain favor, allowing leads to book time directly on your calendar.

Pro Tip: Always send new emails to yourself first and check them on your phone. This way, typos and formatting issues are more accessible to catch, and you'll ensure your email looks clean.

STEP 4
Personalize Every Email

People want emails that speak directly to them and their situation. Personalization goes beyond using someone's name. It's about tailoring the message to their specific needs or actions. HubSpot's Email Marketing Benchmarks report shows that personalized emails can lead to up to 6x higher response rates (HubSpot Blog).

Try This Today:
If someone fills out a form for a mortgage refinance, send them an email with a subject line like "John, Here's How Refinancing Could Save You $500 a Month." The more directly your email addresses their needs, the more likely they will respond.

Pro Tip: Personalize based on their most recent interaction with you. Whether it's a form they filled out or an interest they've shown, use that as the foundation for your message. Most CRMs offer built-in tools to help automate this process.

STEP 5
Avoid the Spam Folder—Set Up Proper Authentication

The worst thing that can happen to your emails is for them to land in spam. Setting up SPF, DKIM, and DMARC ensures that your emails are seen as legitimate and reach your recipient's inbox.

- **SPF (Sender Policy Framework)**: This protocol verifies that your email is sent from an approved server, helping prevent others from spoofing your domain.
- **DKIM (DomainKeys Identified Mail)**: This adds an encrypted signature to your email, proving the content hasn't been tampered with.
- **DMARC (Domain-based Message Authentication, Reporting, and Conformance)**: This combines SPF and DKIM to give email providers instructions on handling messages that fail authentication.

Try This Today:
Your CRM or email platform will guide you through setting up SPF and DKIM. This is a one-time setup that dramatically improves your email deliverability.

Pro Tip: If you're using a new domain, "warm it up" by sending small batches of emails first. Gradually increase the volume over time to build trust with email providers.

STEP 6
Use Automated Sequences to Nurture Leads

Automated email sequences are a powerful way to nurture leads without constantly hitting "send." These sequences can trigger based on lead activity, such as changing their status or filling out a form.

Try This Today:
Set up a simple three-email sequence for new mortgage leads:
- **Welcome Email:** Introduce yourself and what you can offer.
- **Educational Email:** Provide valuable content like "Top 5 Tips for First-Time Homebuyers."
- **Conversion Email:** Offer a free consultation or rate quote to push them to the next step.

Pro Tip: Don't just focus on new leads. Use automation to nurture existing clients with cross-selling opportunities or referral requests.

STEP 7
Track Your Results and keep Tweaking

The best email marketers constantly test and improve. To determine what's working, pay attention to open, click-through, and conversion rates.

Try This Today:
Use A/B testing to try out different subject lines or send times. For example, test "Should You Refi? Get Your Options Today" versus "How Much Can You Save by Consolidating Your Debts?" and see which performs better.

Pro Tip: Regularly remove inactive subscribers to keep your email list clean. This will improve your deliverability and keep your engagement rates strong.

ADVANCED TIPS:
TAKE IT TO THE NEXT LEVEL

Once you've nailed the basics, these advanced strategies can make your email marketing even more impactful.

Behavioral Email Triggers

Use behavioral triggers to send emails based on a lead's actions—like clicking on a specific link or visiting your website. For example, if someone clicks on "mortgage refinancing," send them follow-up emails focused solely on that topic.

Dynamic content

Dynamic content changes based on who's receiving the email. For example, a client interested in refinancing sees personalized rates, while someone interested in purchasing a new home sees different content in the same email. This level of personalization boosts engagement because it feels tailor-made.

WHAT TECHNOLOGY DO YOU NEED?

You'll need the right tools to automate and manage your email marketing to get started.

- **CRM (Customer Relationship Management) Tools:**
  A good CRM helps you manage contacts, track sales stages, and automate email sequences based on lead behavior.

- **Sales Automation Platforms:**
These are more advanced tools that allow you to trigger personalized emails based on specific lead actions, like clicking a link or filling out a form.
- **Email Service Providers (ESPs):**
These platforms let you design emails, set up automation, and track results. Most ESPs include templates and easy-to-use editors, so you don't need a tech team to get started.

Pro Tip: Don't overcomplicate things. Start using the CRM you already have to automate simple sequences based on changing lead statuses. Once you get the hang of it, consider integrating more advanced tools.

START SIMPLE AND LAYER IN COMPLEXITY OVER TIME

You don't need a complex system to succeed with email marketing. Start by sending two weekly emails, segmenting your leads, personalizing your messages, and ensuring your emails are mobile-friendly. Automate what you can track to see what's working and constantly improve.

 By layering in these strategies over time, you'll see more conversions, more referrals, and stronger relationships with your clients—all powered by intelligent, well-executed email marketing.

125

CHAPTER 12

Inbox cinema:
Engaging Your Audience with creative cRM

Cell phones have completely changed how we interact with emails—now, it's all about that instant, on-the-go connection. With smartphones always in hand, emails are no longer something you check on your desktop—they're in your pocket, just waiting to be opened when they arrive. That means mobile users expect quick, easy interactions. They're likely to skim, looking for short, snappy content, bold visuals, and easy-to-tap buttons. Emails must fit into our fast-paced lives, so brands that master mobile-friendly design see higher engagement, quicker responses, and, ultimately, more conversions!

In today's digital world, email marketing still holds much power when building genuine relationships with your audience. But when you combine it with a CRM system, the magic happens. Why? Because it lets you move beyond one-size-fits-all emails. With CRM, you can send personalized, timely messages that turn potential clients into loyal customers— and loyal customers into raving fans who spread the word about your business! Using CRM data, you can connect with your audience on a deeper level, nurture leads, keep customers coming back, and drive long-term success.

But here's the key: It's not just about efficiency and automation. It's about creating meaningful, authentic interactions. An intelligent email strategy powered by CRM lets you send the perfect message immediately, turning casual subscribers into true brand advocates. In this chapter, we'll explore why engaging through emails is so crucial when using a CRM system and how it can transform your marketing, customer relationships, and overall business growth.

Capturing your audience's attention through email isn't always easy. It's more than just delivering the right message—it's about doing it with creativity and strategy. To nail this, you've got to understand the process behind crafting messages that engage and convert.

Let's break it down with some practical, actionable steps:

Know Your Audience

- Research and Analyze: Dig into the data to understand your audience's likes, dislikes, and pain points.
- Create Buyer Personas: Build profiles representing different groups within your audience, focusing on their needs and motivations.
- Engage in Conversations: Ask for feedback! Use surveys, forms, or interviews to better understand what your audience wants.

Segment Your Email List for Personalization

- Group by Behavior: Segment based on past purchases, email interactions, or browsing habits.
- Demographic Segmentation: Tailor your messaging based on age, location, or job role.
- Dynamic Content: Make sure each email feels personalized to the recipient so it speaks directly to them.

Optimize Subject Lines

- Keep It Short and Sweet: Aim for 40-60 characters to keep it mobile-friendly.
- Incorporate Power Words: Use words that spark emotion or action to make your subject line pop.
- A/B Test: Experiment with different subject lines to see which resonates most.

craft a valuable Email Body

- Be Clear and Concise: Get to the point quickly so your message is easily digestible.
- Offer Value: Focus on how your product or service will benefit your audience. What's in it for them?
- Use Visuals Wisely: Include images, GIFs, or videos, but don't overwhelm your reader.

Include a Strong Call-to-Action (cTA)

- Be Specific: Tell your readers exactly what action to take next.
- Make It Stand Out: Use buttons or bold fonts to draw attention.
- Create Urgency: Encourage immediate action with phrases like "limited-time offer" or "act now!"

Test and Analyze Performance

- A/B Testing: Test different elements (subject lines, email copy, CTAs) to see what works best.
- Track Key Metrics: Monitor open rates, click-through rates, and conversions to gauge performance.
- Refine and Adapt: Use what you've learned to improve future campaigns.

By following these steps, you'll create emails that grab attention and inspire action! A CRM system makes the whole process easier, allowing you to manage customer relationships, personalize content, and track metrics for continual improvement.

SUBJECT LINES

Subject lines are a critical component of email marketing within CRM systems, as they serve as the first point of contact between your message and the recipient. A compelling subject line grabs attention and sets the tone for the content inside, directly influencing open rates and engagement. In a CRM system, personalized and optimized subject lines help tailor emails to specific audience segments, ensuring the right message resonates with the right individual. By leveraging data from your CRM, you can continually refine subject lines through A/B testing and performance analysis, driving higher engagement and overall campaign success.

Top-performing email subject lines often include elements that spark curiosity, create urgency, or offer value. Here are some of the most effective types of subject lines to increase open rates:

1. Curiosity-Driven Subject Lines:
   - "You won't believe what happened next..."
   - "This secret could change everything."
   - "Have you seen this yet?"

2. Personalized Subject Lines:
   - "Hey [First Name], this is just for you!"
   - "A special offer for you, [First Name]"
   - "Your personalized update is here, [First Name]"

3. Urgency and FOMO (Fear of Missing Out):
   - "Last chance! Only 24 hours left!"
   - "Hurry! Limited stock available!"
   - "Don't miss out – only a few spots left!"

4. Numbers and Lists:
   - "7 ways to boost your productivity today"
   - "Top 5 tricks for [specific goal]"
   - "The only three tips you need for [desired result]"

5. Offer or Discount-Oriented:
   - "Exclusive: 20% off for today only!"
   - "A deal just for you: Save big on [product]"
   - "Your discount is waiting – grab it now!"

6. Questions to Spark Engagement:
   - "Are you ready to [solve a problem]?"
   - "Want to achieve [desired goal]? Here's how!"
   - "What's stopping you from [taking action]?"

7. Benefit-Focused Subject Lines:
   - "Boost your sales in 3 simple steps"
   - "Get more done with less effort"
   - "Here's how to achieve [specific benefit] today"

8. Curiosity-Piquing Offers:
   - "A surprise gift inside!"
   - "Open for a special offer, just for you"
   - "Unlock your free [resource] now"

9. Emotional Appeal:
- "Feel confident about your next move"
- "Your success starts here"
- "Let's make this your best year yet!"

These subject lines are designed to capture attention and make recipients want to open the email to learn more. Personalization and clear value are crucial to maximizing their effectiveness.

BODY OF THE EMAIL

To be creative and effective in the body of an email using a CRM system, incorporating video can significantly enhance engagement. Here are several strategies that leverage CRM data to craft compelling emails:

- **Dynamic Content Personalization:** Use CRM data to tailor emails with personalized elements like the recipient's name, location, or past interactions. Incorporating customized video content, such as a product recommendation or a personalized message from your team, can make the email more engaging and relevant.

- **Segmented Messaging:** Segment your audience based on behavior, interests, or demographics and send targeted video content that speaks directly to their needs. For example, send tutorial videos to new customers or exclusive product sneak peeks to loyal shoppers.

- **Interactive Video Elements:** Embed clickable videos that encourage interaction. Whether it's a product demo, explainer video, or customer testimonial, videos can drive engagement, while CRM tools track how recipients interact with the content.
- **Visuals and Infographics with Video:** Combine personalized videos with other visuals, such as infographics or charts tailored to specific segments. For instance, a video can explain a service, while personalized graphics show data relevant to that recipient.
- **Clear, Actionable CTAs with Video:** Use videos to guide recipients toward your call-to-action (CTA). For example, a video might end with a strong CTA encouraging viewers to book a demo, claim a special offer, or learn more. CRM data can personalize these CTAs based on the recipient's stage in the customer journey.
- **Behavior-Based Triggered Videos:** Automate email sends triggered by user behaviors like an abandoned cart or recent purchase. These emails could feature personalized video content reminding them of their abandoned items or providing an unboxing video of a product they purchased.
- **Storytelling with Video and Data:** Use CRM insights to craft videos that tell a

personalized story addressing customer pain points or highlighting testimonials from similar clients. Stories brought to life with video can create an emotional connection that resonates.

Incorporating video into your email marketing through CRM data allows you to create personalized, engaging emails that grab attention, spark interaction, and deliver better results.

Email marketing is all about building genuine connections. When combined with CRM, your emails evolve from generic blasts into tailored, timely conversations that resonate. CRM data helps craft relevant emails that turn prospects into loyal customers and customers into passionate advocates.

The key to success lies in creating authentic interactions. By understanding your audience, segmenting messages, and refining your approach, you're not just sending emails but building lasting relationships.

CHAPTER 13

The Nerd Out:
Diving Deep into CRM Customization

For anyone who's spent more than a few weeks in a modern business environment, the words "CRM software" probably evoke curiosity, excitement, and a vague sense of dread. As an experienced user who's wrestled with more CRMs than I'd care to admit, let me guide you through this delightful maze of features, integrations, and the ever-tempting allure of customization options. Buckle up—it's going to be a feature-packed ride!

THE BASICS:
WHAT'S A CRM, AND WHY DO YOU NEED ONE?

First things first, what is a CRM? In its simplest form, a Customer Relationship Management (CRM) system is a tool that helps businesses manage interactions with current and potential customers. Think of it as a supercharged Rolodex that stores contact information tracks every interaction, manages sales pipelines, and can even predict your next move—sometimes better than your mother-in-law.

But why do you need one? Well, suppose you've ever tried to juggle a hundred customer emails, five ongoing deals, three customer complaints, and a partridge in a pear tree. In that case, you'll understand the appeal of having all this information in one place. A good CRM can be your best friend, keeping you organized, efficient, and somewhat saner.

Since my first journey with a CRM in 1998, I have been on an Epic Adventure, trying to find the Best CRM Ever: feature-rich, practical, intuitive, easy to use, accessible, customizable as my business grows, and adapts to industry and technical trends and demands, all without all of the additional expenses. Avoiding high costs is like dodging potholes on a bumpy road—you need to steer carefully, or you'll end up with a wallet that's as empty as a gas tank after a cross-country road trip!

TECHNICAL FEATURES: THE DEVIL'S IN THE DETAILS

Choosing a CRM is like buying a car; everyone's got an opinion, and there are so many options that it's easy to get lost. Let's break down some critical technical features you'll want to consider.

Cloud-Based vs. On-Premise

- **Cloud-Based CRM:** This is the Netflix of CRMs—easy to access, no setup headaches, and you can use it anywhere, even in your pajamas. Cloud-based CRMs like Salesforce or HubSpot are great for businesses that need flexibility and do not want to deal with the IT equivalent of cleaning out the garage.

- **On-Premise CRM:** This is more like owning a DVD collection—higher upfront costs and more control, but be prepared to handle the maintenance. On-premise solutions like Microsoft Dynamics can offer better security and customization, but you'll need an IT team that knows their stuff.

Integration Capabilities

A CRM is only as good as its ability to play nice with others. Can it integrate with your email marketing platform, social media channels, e-commerce site, and that weirdly specific accounting software your CFO or Bookkeeper swears by? Look for CRMs with robust APIs and pre-built integrations, or be prepared to spend some time (and money) on custom development.

You might find a CRM that integrates with your coffee machine if you're lucky. It's not essential, but wouldn't that be a perk?

Automation

Automation is the CRM's version of magic. It can handle repetitive tasks, like sending follow-up emails or updating records, freeing you to focus on more strategic work—like perfecting your office chair swivel. Look for CRMs that offer workflow automation, lead scoring, and automatic data entry. If the CRM can do your job better than you can, you're on the right track.

Reporting and Analytics

If you love data (and who doesn't?), your CRM's reporting and analytics features will be your playground. A good CRM will offer customizable dashboards, real-time reporting, and the ability to track key performance indicators (KPIs) that matter to your business. The best ones will also let you slice and dice your data faster than a sushi chef.

Beware of over-complicating things. I created a detailed dashboard that took three days to load and crashed the system twice. Sometimes, less is more.

Mobile Access

Business doesn't stop just because you're not at your desk. A CRM with a robust mobile app can be a game-changer, allowing you to update leads, check schedules, and close deals while pretending to pay attention to your kid's soccer game. The key here is usability—if the mobile app feels like solving a

Rubik's Cube, keep looking.

CUSTOMIZABILITY: MAKE IT YOURS (BUT NOT TOO MUCH)

Now, let's talk about customization. Every business is unique, and your CRM should be able to adapt to your needs without requiring a PhD in software engineering.

Custom Fields and Layouts

The ability to add custom fields and modify layouts is a must. This allows you to track the data that's relevant to your business. Want to add a field for "Preferred Ice Cream Flavor"? Go for it. Just remember, with great power comes great responsibility. I once went down a rabbit hole and created so many custom fields that it felt like a personality quiz.

Custom Workflows

Workflows are the secret sauce of any good CRM, automating processes like lead routing, deal progression, and customer follow-ups. A customizable CRM will let you design these workflows to match your business processes. Just test them thoroughly— there's nothing like sending a "Welcome" email to a customer who's just unsubscribed.

User Roles and Permissions

Not everyone in your company needs access to everything. A customizable CRM will let you set user roles and permissions so your sales team can't accidentally delete all your leads and your marketing intern, doesn't start tinkering with your financial reports. It's like childproofing your CRM—essential for peace of mind.

custom Reports and Dashboards

We've already talked about reporting, but the ability to create custom reports and dashboards is a crucial customization aspect. You want to see the data that matters to you, whether that's sales performance, customer satisfaction, or how many times Steve from accounting has logged in late this month.

THE FUN STUFF: CRM ADD-ONS AND PLUGINS

Once you've got the basics down, it's time to explore the CRM equivalent of putting a spoiler on your minivan: add-ons and plugins.

Email Marketing Integration

Many CRMs offer built-in email marketing tools, but if you're serious about your campaigns, look for integrations with platforms like Mailchimp or Go High Level. These will give you more options for segmenting your audience, tracking engagement, and automating follow-ups. Plus, you'll have a better excuse for all those "strategic" coffee breaks while your campaign runs itself.

Social Media Integration

Social media is where the action is, and your CRM should be able to track interactions, manage leads, and even automate responses. Some CRMs, like Zoho or Nimble, offer built-in social media tools, while others will integrate with platforms like Hootsuite. Just be careful not to get too caught up in the analytics—you might know more about your followers than your actual friends.

Chatbots and AI Assistants

If you've ever dreamed of having a virtual assistant, now's your chance. Many CRMs now offer chatbot and AI integrations that can handle customer inquiries, schedule appointments, and even upsell products. It's like having a clone but without the awkward conversations.

Gamification

Some CRMs offer gamification features to make the sales process more engaging. Think of it as leveling up, but instead of defeating dragons, you're closing deals. Leaderboards, badges, and points systems can add a fun, competitive edge to your team's performance. Just try not to get too carried away—I once saw a sales rep spend three hours designing a custom badge for "Most Calls Made While Taking An Online Class."

A FEW FINAL WORDS OF WISDOM

Choosing the right CRM is a bit like dating—you need to find one that's a good fit for your needs, won't drive you crazy, and, ideally, won't break the bank. It's easy to get seduced by fancy features and shiny interfaces, but ultimately, it's all about how well the CRM fits your business processes.

Take advantage of free trials, talk to other users, and don't fear walking away if it doesn't feel right. Remember, the goal is to make your life easier, not to spend the next six months in CRM purgatory, crying into your keyboard as you try to configure another custom field.

And if you do find the perfect CRM? Hold onto it, cherish it, and maybe—just maybe—take a moment to appreciate that technology can make our lives easier. Just don't let it get too smug about it.

CHAPTER 14

Elevate Your CRM: Pushing the Boundaries

Customer Relationship Management (CRM) systems have come a long way, changing how businesses connect with customers, streamline processes, and grow. But, with technology moving faster than ever, staying ahead of the curve isn't just important—it's necessary. A modern CRM is more than a contact list. It's an intelligent system that boosts efficiency and helps every department work better.

This chapter explores the future of CRM technology, focusing on AI (Artificial Intelligence) and other up-and-coming trends. We'll discuss how sales, compliance, and other teams can use AI to work smarter. We'll also examine mobile access, voice-to-text, and task automation as key drivers pushing CRMs into the future.

THE AI REVOLUTION: CHANGING THE CRM GAME

AI is a game-changer for CRM. What used to be an essential tool is now an intelligent assistant that helps teams do more with less. AI can help every department run smoother, work faster, and make smarter decisions. Let's explain how AI can take your CRM to the next level.

Sales: Better Leads, Better Timing, Better Engagement

In sales, AI can automate tedious tasks and make managing leads easier. Here's how:

- Lead Prioritization: AI can rank your leads by how likely they are to close based on patterns from past deals. This helps your sales team focus on the leads that matter most.
- Timing Recommendations: AI can suggest the best follow-up times based on email open rates and customer behavior. This gives sales reps the right timing for every touchpoint.
- Personalized Sales Scripts: AI can create custom scripts by analyzing past interactions, helping sales teams connect with prospects more personally.

Compliance: Staying on Top of Rules Automatically

For industries like finance or healthcare, staying compliant is critical. AI helps by:

Monitoring Regulations: AI can monitor regulatory changes and alert your team when new rules are introduced.

Meeting TCPA Standards: AI can search for required terms in conversations based on client location or product type and send alerts if things go off-track.

Automated Alerts: AI can notify team members when compliance tasks need attention, helping you avoid missed deadlines and reduce risk.

Marketing: Sharper Targeting, Smarter Campaigns

AI brings new power to marketing by helping:

- Track Engagement in Real Time: AI analyzes data from sources like Google Ads and social media, letting your team make quick adjustments for better results.
- Lead Scoring: AI tracks user behavior, flags high-interest visitors, and scores them based on conversion likelihood, giving marketers an edge.
- Hyper-Targeting: AI helps create campaigns tailored to specific audiences, ensuring the right message gets to the right people.

Customer Support:
Faster, More Personal Service

AI is also changing customer support by:

- Prioritizing Tickets: AI analyzes each ticket's urgency and importance, ensuring top issues are handled first.
- Automating Follow-Ups: AI sends reminders for unresolved tickets, ensuring no customer gets overlooked.
- Customer Satisfaction Surveys: AI can trigger customized surveys after each support interaction, allowing you to gather feedback and make quick improvements.

Mobile Access:
Always On, Always Connected

Today's workforce isn't stuck in the office. Mobile CRM access means your team can update records, check customer data, and stay in touch—no matter where they are.

- Instant Updates: Sales reps can log details after meetings and even close deals.
- Task Management: Mobile CRMs let employees manage tasks, set reminders, and stay on top of their schedules from anywhere.
- Collaboration: Team members can share updates, documents, and insights no matter where they are, keeping everyone in the loop.

Voice-to-Text: Easier Data Entry, Faster Updates

Instead of typing, voice-to-text lets sales and support teams log real-time updates.

- Capture Real-Time Insights: Reps can verbally log notes after customer interactions, ensuring no detail is missed.
- Save Time: Voice-to-text reduces typing time, letting your team focus on higher-value tasks.
- Improve Accuracy: By logging details right away, there's less risk of missing or forgetting important info.

Pre-Determined Automations: Smoother Workflows

AI-driven automation helps streamline workflows across the board:

- Auto-Assign Tasks: If someone is out, AI can reassign tasks to another team member to keep things running smoothly.
- Automated Email Responses: AI can send auto-replies based on triggers like purchases or unresolved tickets, keeping customers in the loop without extra effort.
- Workflow Automation: AI can automatically move leads through the pipeline, assign tasks, or trigger follow-ups, making your team more efficient.

Adopting these trends is essential to keeping your CRM at the forefront. AI can help automate tasks, analyze data, and drive better decisions, turning your CRM into the hub of your business's success. Moving forward means more than just updating tech. It's about building a culture of innovation that empowers your team, improves productivity, and gives your customers a better experience.

CHAPTER 15

Automate to Dominate: CRM Workflow Automation

In today's fast-paced world, time is money, and every customer interaction counts. With rising expectations, businesses need to streamline their operations, and CRM Automation is a sure way for them to step up. Imagine managing leads, sending out personalized messages, and analyzing data with minimal effort—and without human error. In this chapter, we'll explore the power of CRM Automation, the headaches of doing things manually, and how automation can help you scale your business, keep clients happy, and boost sales.
Let's get into it!

WHY AUTOMATE YOUR CRM?

Let's start by discussing the problems you face without automation. Tasks like sending emails, managing leads, setting up tags, or even generating reports can quickly pile up, eating into your day. It's easy to lose track of follow-ups; when things get busy, that could mean missed opportunities. Simply put, if you're not automating, you leave money on the table. Plus, your CRM can become a mess, making it hard to keep track of what's going on.

By automating, you take your CRM's efficiency up a notch. It saves time, cleans up workflows, and cuts down on mistakes. For example, you can set up an intake system that automatically sorts new clients, sends personalized welcome messages, and ensures your team knows what's happening next. Whether your business is large, small, or between, automation is a game-changer.

When you automate your CRM, expect less stress, easier lead nurturing, and happier clients. Automatic engagement sequences help you build relationships at scale while still feeling personal. You can send customized follow-ups, launch SMS campaigns, and set up timely reminders. The best part? Prospects and clients will believe you're reaching out personally. Trigger-based workflows also keep things rolling by reacting to customer actions and making your outreach feel more natural and relevant.

It doesn't stop there—automation also simplifies the onboarding process for both clients and your team.

You can set up automation that sends instructions, assigns tasks, and guides people step-by-step. Internal processes like lead assignments, task reminders, or updating statuses can be automated, too, making your team more productive without the chaos. It's all about creating a seamless experience so your team and clients feel supported without needing constant hand-holding.

SMS Automation is also crucial for tracking where your leads are coming from. By automating text responses tied to specific campaigns or sources, you can quickly pinpoint which marketing efforts drive the most engagement. This helps you optimize your strategy and allocate resources more effectively. SMS Automation lets you engage leads quickly while providing precise source tracking, making it easy to identify and double down on the most effective channels.

Choosing to automate your CRM is about growth and efficiency. Businesses that embrace CRM Automation tend to see a boost in productivity and customer satisfaction. It frees up time to focus on building long-term relationships rather than being bogged down by daily tasks.

HOW TO LEVERAGE AUTOMATION

Now that we've got the "why" down, let's dive into the "how." CRM workflow automation is one of the best ways to start. Workflows are a series of automated actions that follow predefined triggers. They create personalized journeys for your customers without requiring manual input.

To get going, start small. The key to maximizing automation is to keep things simple and focused. For example, when a new lead enters your CRM, you can set up a workflow to send a welcome message and assign a follow-up task to a team member. This interaction ensures that your lead feels valued from the start. The basics? Pick a trigger (like a form submission), add actions (like sending notifications), and set delays or conditions to personalize the journey. These workflows should align with your company's goals, like automating reminders, delegating tasks, or tracking progress, cutting down the need for manual effort.

Once you've nailed the basics, you can explore more advanced things like conditional logic, decision trees, and action-based triggers. These let you create personalized customer experiences—think follow-up emails for unresponsive leads or customized offers based on their past purchases. This level of personalization helps you engage customers better and increases the chances of converting leads into loyal clients.

To stay ahead, regularly review and tweak your workflows. As your business grows, so should your automation. Look at performance data to spot bottlenecks or areas for improvement. You align your automation with your overall business goals by staying flexible and making data-driven changes.

WHAT'S COMING TO CRM AUTOMATION?

Looking ahead, the future of CRM automation is super exciting, especially with AI taking center stage. Imagine your CRM predicting customer needs before they even ask. That's where intelligent recommendations come in. AI can analyze customer behavior and suggest the right actions to keep them engaged—like reminding you to follow up with a lead who's been quiet or suggesting personalized offers based on past activity. This not only keeps clients happy but also strengthens your relationships.

The future will also involve dynamic workflows that respond in real-time. If a customer shows interest in a specific product or service, your CRM can instantly adapt messaging or strategies to keep them hooked. This level of responsiveness shifts your CRM from a passive tool to an active player in sealing deals and building connections.

Data will also be a significant player in this. Advanced analytics will give you deeper insights, allowing you to fine-tune processes continually. AI will highlight what's working and what's not, helping you improve workflows over time. With every interaction, you'll get smoother and more effective engagements.

Future CRM systems must keep up with customers as they engage across different platforms. Imagine being able to track and interact with a customer, whether they're messaging you on social media, emailing you, or visiting your store. This seamless experience will build loyalty and trust. Integrating all your communication channels into one CRM makes responding quickly to customer inquiries and concerns easier.

Predictive analytics is another game-changer. AI can use historical data to forecast market trends, helping you stay ahead of the curve. You can optimize your outreach by knowing when and how customers will most likely engage.

New technologies like machine learning can take your CRM Automation to the next level. As your system learns from customer interactions, it can refine recommendations and workflows in real-time. This leads to more satisfied clients and positions your business as a leader.

CONCLUSION

The advantages of CRM automation are clear: it saves time, makes things more efficient, and lets you focus on what matters—building relationships with your clients. With intelligent recommendations, dynamic workflows, and powerful analytics, you won't just keep up with competitors; you'll set the standard! Automation empowers your business to respond more to customer needs, ensuring no lead is left behind.

Investing in CRM Automation is necessary in a world where personalization and efficiency are king. As you roll out these strategies, think long-term. The more you automate today, the better positioned you'll be for tomorrow.

Take the plunge, implement these strategies, and watch your business thrive as you turn roadblocks into opportunities. By automating your CRM, you're not just improving processes—you're transforming how you connect with clients and setting yourself up for ongoing success.

Rethink Everything

CHAPTER 16

CRM: The Ultimate Business Partner

In the ever-evolving landscape of business technology, a customer relationship management (CRM) system is no longer optional—it's a must.

Your CRM is more than a tool; it's a business partner that can make or break your operational efficiency, client relationships, and growth potential.

However, choosing a CRM isn't a decision to take lightly.

With so many options on the market, how do you ensure you're picking the right one?

Let's walk through what to look for when evaluating a CRM, using my experience with Go High Level (Go High Level) as an example. Whether you're just starting or looking to upgrade, this chapter will help you avoid the pitfalls and find a CRM that works with you, not against you.

WHAT IS YOUR BUSINESS PROCESS?

Before diving into the world of CRMs, you need to step back and map out your own business process.

- How do your clients interact with your business?
- How would you like them to interact with you and your business?

What's their journey from leading to loyal customers? Mapping this journey is essential because it allows you to identify the tools and functions your CRM must provide.

The next thing to think about: I often encounter business owners whose clients and data are spread across numerous systems—email marketing, appointment booking, invoicing, etc. This fragmentation creates inefficiencies and makes it difficult to manage and scale. Your CRM should act as the central hub that organizes all these moving pieces, streamlining your client management process from start to finish.

For example, with Go High Level, you can manage

leads and clients through sales pipelines, automating tasks. Imagine seeing exactly where every lead is in your sales process, from initial contact to close, with the ability to move them through the pipeline automatically based on specific actions like clicking a link or submitting a form.

This level of organization starts with a deep understanding of your process.

SALES VS. MARKETING CRM

CRMs come in two primary flavors: sales-focused and marketing-focused. Both types serve different purposes, and the right one for your business needs will depend on those needs.

A **sales CRM** helps you manage individual relationships and track where each client is in the buying process. It's about personal connections and ensuring no lead slips through the cracks. For example, in Go High Level, you can create custom pipelines for different types of projects or clients, then use automation to trigger specific actions as clients move from one stage to another. Need to send an email when a deal moves to the 'negotiation' stage? Go High Level does that automatically, allowing you to stay focused on closing the deal rather than getting bogged down in administrative tasks.

A **marketing CRM**, on the other hand, is about managing large groups of people and moving them through broader marketing processes. This involves email campaigns, funnels, and mass communication. In Go High Level, the marketing CRM functions beautifully alongside the sales CRM. You can build sophisticated email campaigns, send SMS messages, and even create intelligent lists to segment your audience based on their actions—such as purchasing a product or attending a webinar. This dual approach allows you to seamlessly manage individual relationships and large-scale marketing efforts.

Combining a Sales and Marketing CRM into one is the best option for a streamlined business.

KEY FEATURES TO EVALUATE IN A CRM

Once you have a clear understanding of your business process, it's time to look at the features any good CRM should offer and the basics of a CRM that you need.

- **Third-Party Integrations**
  No CRM will have every feature you want out of the box, but many offer integrations with other tools to fill the gaps. Does the CRM connect to your existing software? Can it integrate with your email marketing provider, appointment scheduler, or accounting software? If not, does it offer an open API to build custom connections? Go High Level, for example, has an open API, meaning you can integrate it with virtually any tool you need. It also has native integrations for popular platforms like Facebook, Google, and Mailgun.

- cost considerations

  The cost of a CRM is more than just the monthly subscription fee. You must consider what tools it can replace and how it will scale with your business. For instance, Go High Level can replace email marketing software, funnel builders, and social media scheduling tools. This consolidation can save you significant money in the long run. Many businesses pay for five or six separate software tools that Go High Level can handle in one package. As your business grows, so will your CRM needs, so make sure to choose one that can scale with you without breaking the bank.

- Automation capabilities

  Time is money. A CRM that allows for automation can save you both. Look for features like automated follow-ups, triggered actions based on client behavior, and workflow automation that move people through your sales and marketing processes with minimal manual intervention. Go High Level excels here, allowing you to build custom workflows that can handle everything from sending an email after form submission to moving a lead through your sales pipeline based on their activity.

- client communication

  One of the most critical features of a CRM is its ability to centralize your client communication. Can you send emails and SMS messages and even manage social media conversations from within the CRM? Go High Level does all of this, offering multiple channels for client interaction. This makes it easy to keep track of conversations and ensures that no client communication falls through the cracks.

VENDOR REPUTATION AND SUPPORT

A CRM is only as good as the company behind it. Before making a decision, research the vendor's reputation. Are they known for excellent customer service? Do they have a reliable support system in place? For example, I've found their support to be top-notch with Go High Level. They offer live chat, phone support, and a vibrant community where users can get advice and share solutions.

You should also look at how often the CRM is updated. Does the company regularly roll out new features? In today's fast-moving tech world, a CRM that isn't evolving will quickly become obsolete. Go High Level is constantly adding new features, including AI-powered tools that help businesses stay ahead of the curve.

FUTURE-PROOFING YOUR CRM

The pace of innovation in the CRM space is rapid, particularly with advancements in AI. As you evaluate CRMs, consider how future-proof they are. Will they be able to adapt to new technology, or will they be left behind? AKA, do they have the funds to do so?

Go High Level is at the forefront of CRM innovation, particularly its AI features and the ability to integrate with cutting-edge tools.

When choosing a CRM, you're not just solving today's problems but preparing your business for the future.

THE COST OF CHANGE

Choose your forever home, not a starter.

Unlike your first house, starting with a smaller CRM or something that kind of fits will cost you more in the end. So I suggest you choose your forever CRM as soon as you start your business. You will grow into it rather than grow out of it.

Migrating from one CRM to another is a big deal, time-consuming, and will disrupt your business.

So, choosing a CRM you can stick with for the long haul is essential. That transition becomes more manageable if you can consolidate tools and simplify your workflow with a CRM like Go High Level. Before making a decision, think about how the CRM will impact your current workflow and your team and clients. Will it make their lives easier? Will it save you time, money, and frustration down the line?

A CRM should be an investment, not just another monthly expense. If you choose wisely, that investment will save time, increase sales, and improve client relationships.

CONCLUSION

Choosing the right CRM is a decision that will affect your business for years to come.

You can make an informed decision by focusing on your business process first, understanding the difference between sales and marketing CRMs, and carefully evaluating key features like integrations, automation, and support. The goal is to find a CRM that acts as your business partner, streamlining your operations and helping you grow. And while no CRM is perfect, Go High Level comes pretty close.

If you want to see how Go High Level can work for your business, feel free to reach out. I'd love to help guide you through the process and eliminate CRM headaches.

PAMALA DALE

CHECK OUT THE OTHER BOOKS IN THE SERIES

Made in the USA
Monee, IL
12 December 2024

73392740R10095